Beat the Forex Dealer

BEAT THE FOREX DEALER

An insider's look into trading today's foreign exchange market

Agustin Silvani

A John Wiley & Sons, Ltd., Publication

Other Wiley Editorial Offices

John Wiley & Sons Inc., 111 River Street, Hoboken, NJ 07030, USA

Jossey-Bass, 989 Market Street, San Francisco, CA 94103-1741, USA

Wiley-VCH Verlag GmbH, Boschstr. 12, D-69469 Weinheim, Germany

John Wiley & Sons Australia Ltd, 42 McDougall Street, Milton, Queensland 4064, Australia

John Wiley & Sons (Asia) Pte Ltd, 2 Clementi Loop #02-01, Jin Xing Distripark, Singapore 129809

John Wiley & Sons Canada Ltd, 6045 Freemont Blvd, Mississauga, Ontario, L5R 4J3, Canada

Wiley also publishes its books in a variety of electronic formats. Some content that appears in print may not be available in electronic books.

British Library Cataloguing in Publication Data

A catalogue record for this book is available from the British Library

ISBN 978-0-470-72208-4 (HB)

Typeset in 10/12 Times by Laserwords Private Limited, Chennai, India
Printed and bound in Great Britain by TJ International, Padstow, Cornwall, UK

Contents

PART IV   FX TRADING TIPS   73

PART V   DEALER TRADES   117

PART VI   THE FUTURE   143

APPENDIX   TRADING "HOW TO'S"   149

NOTES   177

Acknowledgements

This book required the expert help and contributions of a wide range of friends and colleagues. Special thanks go out to all of the great people at MIGFX, whose hard work and dedication to trading gave rise to this project. I would also like to give special thanks to Richard Hoffman for his help and dedicated research, and to the many industry contacts whose insights proved invaluable. Without you this book would not have been possible.

I would also like to thank the great people at ProRealTime.com for granting me permission to use their fabulous charts. Every trader should visit their website and check out their charting packages, for they are truly top-notch in the industry.

Introduction

Over the years, I have tried to get my hands on every currency trading book that I could find, but as you may well know the pickings are slim when it comes to FX literature. Apart from a few notable exceptions, most of the available material seems to fall into one of two categories: unabashedly theoretical or completely misguided. The dry, outdated, and sometimes esoteric academic works tend to leave the reader with the perception that currency trading is as gentlemanly and ordered as the world of stamp collecting, when in reality nothing could be further from the truth in a market referred to as a "slaughterhouse" where traders routinely get "chopped up". The FX market I know is one of egos and money, where millions of dollars are won and lost every day, and phones are routinely thrown across hectic trading desks. This palpable excitement has led to the emergence of a second class of literature, often misleading and downright fraudulent, where authors promise the reader riches by offering to make forex trading "easy".

Well, I'll let you in on a little secret: there is nothing easy about trading currencies. If you don't believe me, then stop by Warren Buffet's office and ask him how he could lose $850 million betting on the dollar or ask "King" George Soros why his short bets lost him $600 million not once but *twice* in 1994. Don't these guys read FX trading books? If these investment legends can lose billions in the FX market, what makes anyone think there is anything easy about it?

The average retail trader must feel a terrible disconnect between what is described by famous "experts" and their actual trading experiences. Theory very rarely translates into fact when it comes to trading, and real-life FX trading is much more complicated and tricky than any guru would have you believe. In this jungle it is a kill-or-be-killed attitude that marks survival, and the minute you step on to the playing field a target has been placed next to your account number.

Realizing that most FX books in print are either written by scam artists or academics with little real-world trading experience, I decided to put my own thoughts to paper. While I certainly do not proclaim to be any sort of market wizard, the market insights I have gained while managing a successful currency fund should prove valuable to readers, even if they are just starting their trading careers. Being a firm believer in the "small is beautiful" mantra, I have therefore tried to keep this book short, and to the point.

The purpose of this book is two-fold. First, by explaining the day-to-day mechanics of the FX market and pointing out some of the more unsavory dealings going on in the retail side, I hope to make evident for the reader the risks and rewards involved in currency trading. The second objective of the book is to help turn average traders into winning traders. "Average" traders are losing traders; winning traders are in fact quite rare. However, by highlighting some market-proven trading tricks and techniques, I hope to give traders an initial leg-up.

As you may have guessed, this book takes its name from Edward O. Thorp's landmark work on blackjack, *Beat the Dealer*. In 1962, the MIT mathematics professor revealed to the public the gambling industry's tricks and traps, while at the same time managing to teach a successful method for playing the game of twenty-one. Likewise, you will find this book roughly split into two parts: the first half is dedicated to revealing the foreign exchange market's unfair practices and the second half is designed to help the retail FX trader implement an effective and winning game plan by providing trading tips and detailed examples.

FROM VEGAS TO WALL STREET

The past five years has seen the FX market open its arms to nontraditional participants, and now everyone from dotcom investors to cash-strapped grandmas are jumping in hoping to strike it rich.

What most of these new participants fail to realize is that they are stepping on to a battlefield littered with the remains of day traders and genius "systems". It is frequently noted that over 90% of FX traders do not survive in the long run, yet you won't find that statistic in any of the publicity dished out by the FX brokers. To be profitable, retail traders must realize that the foreign exchange market was fundamentally developed as a professional's market, and its outdated conventions and procedures mean that it still is very much geared toward the professional. In a market where the retail trader exerts little (though growing) influence, most can have little hope of success.

The retail brokers who have sprung up recently would like you to believe that currency trading is a high form of financial speculation. In reality, the average client's trading approach combined with the unscrupulous practices of some brokers make spot FX trading more akin to the games found on the Vegas strip than to anything seen on Wall Street. The new breed of on-line FX brokers simply share too many of the traits employed by casinos to stack the odds in their favor, including these:

- The "house" always has the advantage (the spread).

- The "house" feeds off the player's greed and actively promotes it (by offering trading signals, excessive leverage, and fancy platforms resembling slot machines!).

- The "house" adopts various dubious risk-management controls, which include cheating and cutting off winning players.

All of these benefits ensure that, in the long run, the house (broker) will end up with virtually all of the player's (trader's) money. The odds are simply stacked in their favor.

Thorp's original *Beat the Dealer* was brilliant in that he focused his energy on a niche game (blackjack) which featured changing odds. In a game with fixed odds (such as the lottery) a player is virtually assured ruin, while a game with shifting odds allows the smart player to effectively control his risk while maximizing his gains. Although the long-run odds may not favor the player, a set of rules can be adopted that allow the gambler to "play" only when the odds are in his favor, thus greatly improving his chance for success. Playing in this way enables you to refrain from gambling (betting on luck) and concentrate on playing the probabilities. FX traders need to take a cue from their card-playing counterparts and learn to trade only when the odds are shifted in their favor. In this spirit, the last part of this book is dedicated to exposing high-probability trades commonly seen in the intra-day FX market, which can effectively be used to "double up" when they are seen.

BEAT THE DEALER

In my experience, most retail FX traders seem to have a decent system or genuine "feel" for the market, yet more often than not they still find themselves posting steady losses. They see the possibility for greatness, yet they are unable to grasp it. Something must be missing . . . but what? Although they may spend hours dutifully studying technical analysis, candle charting, and the history of the market, seldom do they take a moment to concentrate on their number one killer: the forex dealer. By preying on the small speculator, these shadowy characters are often single-handedly responsible for turning winning trades into losers.

Both casinos and FX brokers have an ace up their sleeve which ensures that the odds are always shifted aggressively against a player, and not surprisingly these villains share a common name. Dealers are much more than simple order-processors (do you want to buy/sell, hit/stay?); they are in fact the house's fail-safe device sent out to take down any player who is deemed to be winning "too much". Their direct and purposeful interference can ruin even the most advanced or elegant trading system.

Have you ever had your stop hit at a price that turned out to be the low/high for the day? Bad luck perhaps? Maybe. What if it happens more than once? Do you ever feel like the market is "out to get you?" Well, guess what . . . in this zero-sum game it absolutely is.

Dealers make particularly tough opponents for traders because they act on better information. Although it is hard to bluff when the other party knows your cards, you *can* however profit by betting on their actions, and a dealer's actions are, after all, very predictable. You know what they want (your money) and you have a rough idea of how they will come after it (running stops, shading prices, fading moves, etc.); all that you now need is a way to exploit these actions. Throughout this book you will find information meant to help you identify and counteract typical dealer traps, which if implemented correctly can instantly improve your trading profits. Many of these are exactly the same techniques used by hedge funds and CTAs to exploit loopholes left by their dealers, which can also be used successfully by the retail trader.

Make no mistake about it. There is a lot of money to be made in currency trading; you just have to know where to look. Sidestepping dealer traps is one simple way of improving your daily P/L, but it is surely not the only one. Successful trading comes down to taking care of the details, and for me the only way to do this is by providing concrete, up-to-date, real-life examples, and sharing the FX trading tips that have proved so profitable over the years.

In the end, it is my hope that by stripping away the theory and getting down to the core of trading you too may find yourself well on your way to beating the forex dealer!

Some Terms Commonly Used In This Book

Individual (Retail) Trader Nonprofessional trader; i.e. speculates for his own account as opposed to trading for a bank or hedge fund. Normally trades small sizes (under $1 million), usually either for speculation or fun.

Interbank Market Loose term used to describe the FX trading done by banks directly with each other, as opposed to trading with clients. Can essentially be thought of as the "wholesale" FX market, where entry is restricted to professionals. Not a physical market or exchange, the interbank market is a web of credit facilities built over time and used by banks to trade with each other directly or through electronic matching platforms such as Reuters and EBS.

Retail FX Broker Also called Futures Commission Merchant (FCM), these are companies created to "open up" the spot currency market to the retail trader through their small minimum account sizes (as low as $300). In theory, they should simply be the middlemen between the FX wholesalers and their retail client base, charging a small fee (the spread) for their service. Much like on-line stock brokers (E-trade, etc.), they promise to "connect" the retail trader to the market at reduced costs, yet often fall well short of this promise.

FX Dealer If the interbank is the wholesale market and the brokers are the middlemen, then the dealers are the salesmen. Dealers typically work for FCMs or banks, and their primary responsibility is to process client transactions (buy/sell orders). If wanting to trade, clients have the option of phoning their dealer or trading electronically. The dealer then goes to the wholesale market, executes the order, and keeps the price difference (in theory at least). Retail dealers concern themselves mostly with providing accurate prices (through their on-line trading platforms), handling client flows, and running stops of course!

Simplistic view of a retail FX transaction

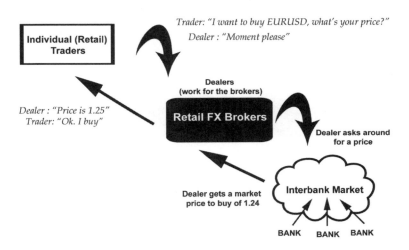

Note. If you are not at all familiar with the foreign exchange market or trading in general, then you may well benefit from reading up on the subject before proceeding. There are many valuable books that teach technical analysis, candlestick reading, history of the markets, economic theory, etc. Most of those books give the beginning trader a basic grounding in the financial theory that underpins successful trading, and should be dutifully studied by all traders; this book is not meant to replace any of them. The material covered in this book is strictly centered on sharing professional "buy-side" insights for trading the spot foreign exchange market.

THROUGH THE EYES OF A TRADER

1
On Markets

If one believes in a random universe, a strong case can be made for the fact that any sort of technical analysis and trading tactics are in fact quite useless. Under this scenario, random and unpredictable price movements makes research, analysis, and market timing an exercise in futility, and relegates any kind of strategy (other than buy-and-hold) to a game of chance, not skill. As Burton Malkiel famously noted, "A blindfolded monkey throwing darts at the financial pages of a newspaper can select a portfolio that will do just as well as one carefully selected by the experts". This market view is supported by the fact that the vast majority of mutual funds fail to beat the broader market year after year, and history shows us that the ten best-performing funds in any one year will drop to the bottom of the pack in the following two to four years, meaning that a manager's outperformance is largely the product of luck, like a gambler's short-term winning streak. Simply put, there is no way to consistently beat the market.

Needless to say, this view of things does not sit well with Wall Street, which preaches that research, analysis, and relying on expertise are the keys to investing (and their business model!). Assuming that we can draw a similar parallel to other markets, then why bother trading? Why spend so much time researching the market and analyzing prices when we could just as simply close our eyes and buy or sell?

Thankfully for traders, although the random walk theory paints a strong case against mutual funds, it is not entirely bullet-proof. Investors consistently fall prey to fear, envy, overconfidence, faddism, and other recognizably human imperfections that make markets not only inefficient but predictably inefficient. In the short run, recognizable patterns *are* indeed visible in the stock market. Bubbles are created, and then burst. If the DOW goes up one week, it is more likely to go up the next week. In the long run all of these moves smooth themselves out, but in the short run, predicting and trading these constant adjustments can actually make for quite a profitable proposition. Through research and analysis we can visually identify these inefficiencies and market anomalies in charts, and then trade their

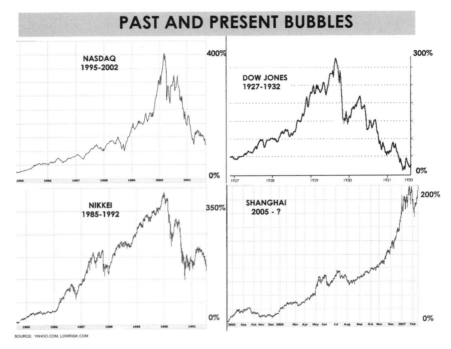

PAST AND PRESENT BUBBLES

SOURCE: YAHOO.COM, LOWRISK.COM

Stock market bubbles tend to be of similar length, duration, and size. The chart patterns are similar since the impetus behind them is the same (low borrowing costs, greed, and overconfidence). "This time it's different...."

expected outcomes. The point in trading is therefore not to forecast the future events themselves, but rather to predict and profit from their consequences instead.

The day the financial community realized exactly how imperfect a science it practices was 19 October 1987. On this "Black Monday" US stock markets managed to drop an incredible 22.6 % for no apparent reason, which proved especially shocking to the brilliant mathematical minds that had spent their academic careers solving most of the puzzles surrounding proper pricing and valuation. By the late 1980s it seemed that markets had finally been "figured out" and trading was no longer the realm of risk-hungry cowboys as technology quickly came to replace the gut in pricing (and trading) decisions. Yet in light of all this, the world's biggest and most sophisticated market still managed to shed nearly one-quarter of its value in *one day* and on no news, putting into question even the most basic financial assumptions. By noon of that day, IBM's stock stopped trading in the face of only sell orders; literally no one wanted to buy. If a stock is only worth as much as someone is willing to pay for it, did this mean that IBM's stock was, at least for the time being, worthless? What exactly was going on? How could we call the market rational and efficient, let alone figured out?

The fact that this event now seems as distant as the stock market crash of 1929 is evidence of just how much we have moved forward, yet many of the underlying reasons behind the crash are still around today and the trading lessons behind these underline the major differences from what we may call the "academic" view of markets and the trader's view.

A LITTLE MARKET THEORY

As we know, professors love formulae, and perfect formulae make for perfect markets. The problem with this kind of oversimplified interpretation of the market is that it tends to marginalize an individual's contribution, while traders realize that sometimes individual actions are actually the driving force behind markets. Why did people sell on Black Monday? It was because everyone else was selling; it is as simple as that.

The problem for the academic world is that while real risks (interest rates, stock prices, etc.) are easy enough to understand, *perceived* risks are much harder to quantify and are therefore generally ignored. After all, how on earth can we measure Joe Investor's sensitivity to risk when on the one hand he spends days researching and analyzing which car to buy and on the other hand he buys Pets.com stock on a friend's tip?

Over the years traders have learned to get a grasp on this tricky subject, and some interesting things about the perception of risk have emerged. We know that risk tolerance decreases once the market is fully invested, which is why asset bubbles build up slowly and deflate violently. We also know that our brain is hard-wired to shy away from pain and regret, thus making us sell our winning stocks while holding on to losers hoping that they will turn around. How many dead internet stocks do you still have in your portfolio?

What we now know is that markets are efficient, but they are not perfectly efficient. The point where buyers and sellers meet does not always reflect "equilibrium", and the sheer number of arbitrage-hungry hedge funds out there can be taken as an indication of the market's imperfection. Since prices are man-made creations that reflect our biases as much as they do economic reality, markets may stay in a state of disequilibrium for a long time when the very reason for buying (prices going up) in turn leads other people to buy.

Those used to doing the day-to-day dirty work in the markets, the traders, dealers, and "locals" in the pit, have all come to realize that at least in the short run, markets are often manipulated and highly irrational. Psychology matters, fear matters. Momentum often trumps economic fact, and we can be fairly certain that as long as there is human involvement in the financial markets they will continue to exhibit the same erratic behavior patterns as human beings. Logic often takes a back seat to greed and fear since at the end of the day it is the trader/money manager that has his job and bonus to look after.

1920's BULL MARKET vs. 1980's BULL MARKET

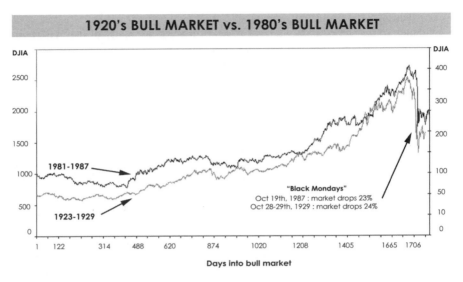

Days into bull market

"A perfect market thinks only of the future, not the past." The market may not have a memory, but traders certainly do. The eerie similarity between the crash of 1929 and 1987 can probably be attributed to traders in 1987 using the past as a way of predicting the future, unwittingly creating a self-fulfilling prophecy with their actions. (Source: Lope Markets)

Traders that overlook these behavioral aspects end up in trouble when confronted with tumultuous and emotional markets, even if for a brief period of time; hence there is the famous saying, "The market can stay irrational longer than you can stay solvent". This saying is more true that you can imagine, and the Wall Street graveyard is littered with traders that made money trading rational markets 99 % of the time, yet got wiped out by that irrational 1 %.

Legendary hedge fund manager Julian Robertson found out just how dangerous it can be to fade[1] irrational markets when he rationally shorted the tech bubble of the 1990s and turned his stellar $22 billion dollar fund into a mere $6 billion basically overnight. His farewell letter to investors pretty much says it all:

> The key to Tiger's success over the years has been a steady
> commitment to buying the best stocks and shorting the worst. In a
> rational environment, this strategy functions well. But in an irrational
> market, where earnings and price considerations take a back seat to
> mouse clicks and momentum, such logic, as we have learned, does not
> count for much.

---

[1]To fade a move is to trade against the prevailing direction. Fading a move higher would mean selling short into the rally.

From a trader's perspective, this means that the market is always right. If irrational investors make a bundle on the way up, while rational investors lose their shirts shorting the move, then who is rational and who is not? Markets are not rational or irrational, they just are, and the only view that traders will ever hold sacred is their need for volatility, because it holds the key to their profits. As long as people are buying and selling, short-term speculators are indifferent as to the rationale behind the moves because they know there is money to be made on both sides of any trade. All that traders care about is maximizing their profits by positioning themselves in advance of the next move, while academics often miss the forest for the trees by being so far removed from the trading floors of the world.

2
The Currency Market

Foreign exchange trading has essentially been around since the advent of money, and although the mechanics have advanced somewhat since the time of the money-changers in the temple, it still boils down to the exchange of one currency for another.

Of all financial markets, the FX market can probably be considered to be among the most "pure" in the sense that supply and demand (in the free-floating currencies) is strictly what determines prices. For the most part, the market is unregulated and free of distorting red tape, and the sheer size of the trading volume means that government intervention has little long-term effect on prices. After all, in a market that trades over $2 trillion a day government intervention can only go so far, and at the end of the day it is the two hundred thousand traders around the world that act as Adam Smith's invisible hand in guiding prices.

Since a market this free and liquid is typically hard to out-guess, you would be right to think: "is it even worth trading such an efficient market?" The good news for traders is that the FX market is not as efficient as it may first appear, and the root of this inefficiency can be traced back to the participant's motivation. The FX market has never been a value creator, but rather a vehicle for other transactions. A US portfolio manager buying Japanese stocks or an Italian company acquiring raw materials from Brazil both inadvertently become FX participants, yet the currency part of their transactions are not usually motivated by profit. The portfolio manager simply needs the yen to buy the stocks and the company needs dollars to buy the coffee.

This type of behavior breeds inefficiencies eagerly exploited by more active market participants, and fortunately for FX traders small arbitrage opportunities still abound. Although the market may be very efficient at giving you a price, whether that price is an accurate reflection of the currency's true "value" is another story altogether, which is why good analysis and trading techniques do pay off in the long run.

Research and analysis in FX proves valuable because the currency market *is* different than Wall Street. The interbank market is by no means a perfect market since information is not freely available, market access is restricted, manipulation takes place, governments intervene, and a large number of participants routinely buy and sell irrespective of profit, which all comes together to turn conventional trading wisdom (such as "let your winners run, cut losers short") on its head in this mostly range-bound market. The FX market is different than other markets, and if you can find a way to recognize, predict, and exploit these imperfections, then there is a great deal of money to be made. Profitable trading strategies do exist and can be found.

A SELECT CLUB

Off-balance sheet earnings are the declared aim of most banks, and spot dealing in FX, which presents high loss potential (as far as price is concerned) but practically no credit risk, falls directly into this category. To understand a bank's motivation for getting involved in this market, all you have to know is that by combining a large FX dealing desk with a decent prop trading group, pretty soon you will be talking about billions in profits. These types of numbers have long made FX the playground of only the biggest and baddest global banks, and because at its core the FX market continues to be a credit market, their dominance is unlikely to be challenged any time soon.

➤ The Big Boys of FX

Out of the 6,322 institutions polled (totaling over $85 trillion in turnover), ten banks were responsible for more than three quarters of all FX turnover.

Marketshare

1. Deutsche Bank 19.26%
2. UBS 11.86%
3. Citigroup 10.39%
4. Barclay's Capital 6.61%
5. RBS 6.43%
6. Goldman Sachs 5.25%
7. HSBC 5.04%
8. Bank of America 3.97%
9. JPMorgan Chase 3.89%
10. Merrill Lynch 3.68%

Source: Euromoney FX Poll. May 2006

Unlike other markets, an FX transaction is not the exchange of cash for another asset (stocks or oil, for example), but rather the exchange of cash today in return for the acceptance of cash at a later date. The interbank market operates on this somewhat unusual principle, where one party depends on the other to meet their obligation without extending credit to each other. As you may well imagine, when dealing in this way it is crucial to know that your counterparty is of the highest credit standing, lest you be left holding the bag on one side of the transaction. For this reason, big banks prefer to deal with big banks, and smaller fish are essentially shut out of the FX pond. As a result, a small group of commercial and central banks (you can call it a cartel if you wish) has always handled the majority of FX turnover with each other, and for each other.

Technology has managed to open up this tight-knit group somewhat, although not to the extent that you may think. Most banks now either operate their own electronic dealing platforms or provide liquidity to a matching system/prime brokerage platform. Products from EBS, Currenex, FXAll, etc., enable banks to reach a larger client base while still maintaining full control over their risk, yet in the end, who do you think owns most of these platforms anyway? The reality is that the same small group of banks still controls the FX market.

AN UNFAIR PLAYING FIELD

From the very beginning, the FX market was designed to ensure that market "insiders" had a considerable edge over market "outsiders". Because of the tight-knit nature of the market and its lack of regulation, the FX market is a fundamentally unfair market for the nonprofessional to operate in. For example, in some emerging countries a Citibank or UBS may be the only game in town, so anyone wanting to trade that currency is forced to "pay up" to play in their turf. A player's positioning on the FX food chain depends on his/her access to information and speed, and with no central clearing exchange, it can be difficult for nonprofessionals to gain access to this information and come up with an accurate view of the market. More often than not, this leaves those with limited access to information at the mercy of their bank dealer.

This is where the FX world differs from traditional financial markets, and things deemed illegal in most other markets are simply regarded as "part of the game" in FX. Insider trading, front running, price shading, etc., are all regularly seen in FX trading, and have absolutely no legal repercussions.

No government oversight and no central dealbook to compare trades means that banks are pretty much free to do whatever they want to their unsuspecting customers. Unlike exchange-traded markets (NYSE) where a market maker has a responsibility to quote the same price to two different parties, an FX dealer may quote his clients whatever price he wishes. Spreads mysteriously widen and shrink, and the "who's who" factor dominates. Good customers receive decent prices (a salesman will shout to the dealer "good price, mate!"), but for irregular or complicated clients it becomes practically impossible to receive fair market prices. God forbid that the dealer "read" you correctly and guessed your intentions (try calling up your dealer and ask him "I wish to buy, what's the price on euro-dollar?"). An FX trader who did not want to get ripped off before had to place 5 to 10 calls to different banks and take their average as the "fair" market price. These inefficiencies, of course, all play into the hands (and pockets) of the brokers.

Dealers are free to behave in this way because they are very often the only game in town, and they know that there is not much customers can do about it. In the same way that you and I knowingly get ripped off by the exchange booth guys at the airport, traders know they are getting short-changed but often have little recourse. If Goldman is the only one willing to take your trade at that moment, you can either take it or leave it; it is as simple as that.

3
A Rare Breed

Putting aside all arguments about efficient markets, traders are around for one thing and one thing only: to make money from their views on the market. Although theory states that investors should not be capable of beating the market in the long run, people like Paul Tudor Jones[1] are happy to go against conventional wisdom by consistently beating the market year after year. Either their success is merely the result of a statistical fluke or great traders are simply a breed apart.

The mark of a great trader is their ability to walk the walk and talk the talk. While most people actually find that on paper they make great trading decisions, when real money becomes involved they soon lose the upper hand. That is because as soon you enter the market, you become emotionally attached to your position and the switch from paper profits to real dollars and cents clouds your thinking by inserting doubt into your reasoning. Think about the past investment decisions you regret the most. They usually involve sound investments that you pulled the plug on too soon (I knew I should have held on to that property in Florida!) or never entered into (I knew I should have bought the Google IPO!). Either way, the error in judgment is frequently caused by the emotional rush brought on when switching from percentages to greenbacks. This mental toughness is the reason great traders are often referred to as having ice-water running through their veins or having private parts made out of steel.

Trading is one of the few professions that enable you to quantify exactly how good you are, since all it takes is a quick glance at your P/L. How does a consultant/engineer/manager know they are good at what they do? Usually it is through a combination of peer respect, promotions, and recognition that they use for measurement. And how do they know if they had a good or bad day? Traffic? Problems

---

[1] Part of the University of Virginia hedgies, started Tudor Investment in 1985. Never a down year, the worst performance was in 2000, when Tudor BVI Global Portfolio fund delivered 11.6 %. Of note, he managed to time the October 1987 market crash and turn it into a 210 % gain.

with suppliers? Now imagine being able to look at your screen at the end of your shift and let *it* tell *you* how your day was. For traders, the measuring stick is simple: money. The more you make, the better you are at your job. If you made more than the guy to your right that must mean that you are better at your job than he is, and if you lost money today that means you had a bad day at work. This turns trading floors into pure meritocracies, and those that make money have the power, while those that don't are soon out the door.

Unlike investing, where the focus is on creating wealth (e.g. dividends), traders make money by catching short-term moves for quick gains. Trading, like poker, can be described as a zero-sum game. If you are winning then someone else must be losing. This battlefield aspect to the markets is something that the novice trader disregards at his/her own peril, since humans sit behind those trading screens and you can bet that they will do everything in their power to take your money, even if that means bending the rules in their favor.

The fact that most traders are also avid gamblers should come as no surprise, and thus you may find at any one time that bets on sporting events or the eating capacity of the latest intern overshadow any market activity on the desk. Another interesting quality about traders is that proficiency with numbers does not automatically translate into positive trading results, and over the years you find great minds like Sir Isaac Newton losing fortunes in the market while atypical participants, such as novelist Julius Verne, become great stock pickers. The ability to look beyond the obvious facts and figures, to think of the market not only from an objective standpoint but also from a subjective view, is what sets great traders apart. *Average traders look to the left-side of the chart, great traders look to the right.*

THE TRADER'S EDGE

A trader's edge is their ability to deal with uncertainty at minimum risk, which is exactly how the Rothschild family made their fortune in the 18th century. The idea was simple yet brilliant: in a time of slow communications, courier pigeons could be used to transmit gold prices across the English Channel, giving you a day's head start on the market and opening the door to arbitrage opportunities. When the price was lower in Paris, they would purchase it there and sell it in London, keeping the difference. Their advantage was information, which was thoughtfully transformed into profits.

Dealing with uncertainty can also mean being pro-active and forcing your opponent's hand. When asked about his playing, Ed Lasker, one of the greatest chess players of all time, noted that in order to succeed he would ask himself, "What is my opponent's present state of mind, and how can I worry him the most?" Similarly, the very best traders have the innate ability to look at the market objectively while at the same time perceiving it from the eyes of their opponents. What move do they fear the most? What will they do if prices go down? Lasker explained that he "sometimes achieved victory by boring my opponents to death, or by luring

them into attacks when attacks weren't in their nature". Successful traders apply
these same concepts on a day-to-day basis, and use this edge to actively shape their
future by playing to their opponent's weaknesses.

Market participants (and pawn shops) know that it is much easier to rip-off
someone in trouble than to make money through your own trading skills, so over
the years they have evolved into efficient killing machines that would make Darwin
proud. If the market catches a wisp of a hedge fund in trouble, you can be sure

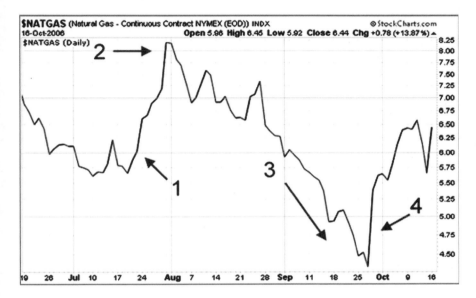

How to lose $6 billion in two months.

1.   Anticipating higher natural gas prices, hedge fund Amaranth places huge bets
         through bullish spread plays.

2.   At this point, the big bets are actually deep in the black and the fund begins to cash
         in on some of their positions. The sudden flood of supply gets the market's attention,
         and the NYMEX boys soon realize that Amaranth is sitting on a huge long position.
         Liquidity dries up and the market begins to turn as the fund desperately tries to get
         out of their trade.

3.   The selling soon snowballs into a rout and natural gas prices fall 50 % in two months.
         Fundamentals are pushed aside as traders move in for an easy play, and word of the
         fund's trouble begins to leak out to the public.

4.   By late September Amaranth is wiped out. The friendly financial community gladly
         offers to "bail them out" by buying their positions at heavily discounted prices. Not
         surprisingly, once the bloodbath is over the market returns to normal trading and
         the sweethearts that bailed them out cash in their positions for great gains.

that the sharks will move in and actively push the market against them until they are dead in the water. This active "hunting" role is something that most model developers do not take into account, and to a large degree it can be said that their "sigma-nine"[2] events are often self-perpetuated. If Amaranth had not gone balls-out long on natural gas, for example, the market would probably not have dropped like it did.

FOREX TRADERS

Foreign exchange speculators are often regarded by developing nations as "economic war criminals" who prey on the weak and defenseless, yet ask FX traders and they will tell you that they are simply the instruments of global macroeconomic forces. As George Soros famously proclaimed, "As a market participant, I don't need to be concerned with the consequences of my [financial] actions." In other words, he did not create the imbalance, so why should he be blamed when he corrects it?

Forex traders are a unique brand of speculator with an almost monastic devotion to their profession, working obscene hours and concerning themselves with global macro events. What effect will the Tokyo earthquake have on the Swiss franc? How will the US dollar react to inflationary signs coming out of Germany? Try explaining how you make a living to a stranger (or your spouse) and they will look at you as if you are crazy. The ability to select, process, and take advantage of seemingly unrelated and unending data points in the blink of an eye is what sets currency traders apart. Through the eyes of a forex trader every asset trade is essentially a bet on exchange rates, and those that learn to connect the dots faster than anyone else end up on top.

The world's economies are now one giant interconnected machine, and the grease that keeps the gears running smoothly is foreign exchange. Legendary FX traders have made their careers by figuring out, before anyone else, what repercussions event X will have on country Y's currency. This clairvoyance often instills a level of self-confidence that would humble professional athletes, and when combined with the tremendous amounts of leverage available to traders it often leads to some truly mind-boggling bets.

In 1988, for example, when Bankers Trust hotshot Andrew Krieger was asked about his short Kiwi position he famously replied, "How large is the monetary supply of New Zealand?" Believe it or not, through the use of derivatives Krieger managed at one point to actually short *more* than New Zealand's entire monetary supply! Although this gutsy bet ended up netting him a cool $300 million, when self-confidence turns into arrogance the effects can be devastating.

---

[2] Nine standard deviations away from the mean, or basically a statistically impossible event.

Why is it a bad idea to give your star trader the keys to the backoffice?

The trading world is filled with stories of one-man demolition crews often referred to as "rogue traders". Here are some of the most infamous:

Yasui Hamanaka. The Sumitomo Corp. trader's positions were so huge, that he earned the nickname "Mr. 5%" for allegedly controlling five percent of the world's copper market. Unfortunately for Sumitomo, his 10 year career was mostly filled with bogus contracts and fictitious entries meant to hide his mounting losses. By the time he was discovered, he had racked up $2.6 billion in losses which he paid for by doing eight years in jail.

Nick Leeson. Star trader for Barings Bank, his derivative losses hidden in his secret 88888 account ended up costing the "Queen's Bank" $1.2 billion and managed to bring down one of the world's most venerable banking institutions overnight.

John Rusnak. Allied Irish Bank's chief rogue trader. His out-of-control fx trades ended up costing the bank a cool $691 million.

Peter Young. Morgan Grenfell's star trader is not best remembered for his unauthorized trades (a mere $350m), but the fact that he showed up to court wearing women's clothes in an attempt to plead insanity. Seems like Young got the last laugh since the court declared him unfit for trial!

4
FX Dealers

To understand how dealers trade, you simply have to understand how dealers think (i.e. make money). If the big banks are the FX wholesalers, then dealers are the salesmen trusted to push their inventory. Like the used car salesman who wants to clear his lot, FX dealers are looking to move as much inventory as possible ("chopping wood" in dealer speak) and regularly adjust their profit margins here and there in order to accomplish this. It may be worth accommodating a transaction for a customer at a slightly lower commission (or loss) if it means locking up business from that client in the future.

Because of the wheeling-and-dealing style of their work, dealers have historically been more associated with the streets of Brooklyn than any Ivy League school, and they are renowned for being quick on their feet and excelling at order-flow trading; they are the definition of the intra-day trader.

ALWAYS BE FADING

A dealer's motto. Market moves are rarely one-way and dealers understand that the majority of the time intra-day markets are range-bound (around 80 %), so any sharp move (gap) is likely to be faded by dealers who have the deep pockets and knowledge that the price will eventually come back to them ... at least most of the time!

Another favorite trading rule of the spot dealer is to never trust the first price. After a news release, dealers know that the first price print is the knee-jerk reaction of the market and most often wrong, so dealers routinely use news events to flush out any weak positions by moving the market against them. This is commonly known as the "head fake," whereby the price moves sharply in one direction before reversing course, catching many traders off-guard in the process.

Dealers always fade the first move; hence the saying "never trust the first price."

CAN DEALERS LOSE MONEY?

Yes. A dealer's biggest nightmare is a runaway market, where they are forced to either stop quoting prices (and risk losing customers) or continue taking the other side of the trade and risk being stuck with a losing position. Prices can at times run away from a dealer so quickly that they are unable to offset their exposure, and leaves the stressed-out dealer with positions deep underwater. Many risk-hungry dealers that continued to quote prices during the USDJPY crash of 1998, for example, were wiped out. In general, any one-way market is bad for dealers, since prices do not retrace and they are forced to eventually unload their positions at a loss. However, from a dealer's perspective, this is simply seen as the "cost of doing business."

TRADERS VERSUS DEALERS

Like two heavyweights in the ring, traders and dealers regularly duke it out in the markets, with speculators complaining about dealers committing "highway robbery" through their quotes and fills, and dealers complaining about traders "picking them off" in arbitrage opportunities. Both have valid points in this love–hate relationship (actually mostly hate), but in the end one cannot do without the other. As in any business, good market contacts and relationships are fundamental to success in the market, and a trader may put up with a dealer's shoddy quotes if he knows he can count on him to take a large CADJPY order on a Friday afternoon, for example. You can have the best ideas in the world, but if you cannot find a counterparty to take your trade then you are going to be stuck with just that: an idea.

Of course, having a good relationship does not mean you are not willing to take the other party's money. Every time a trader picks up the phone to deal, he knows that the person on the other end of the line is going to try to rip him off, but smart traders also routinely play tricks on their brokers. A favorite FX trick was to leave small stops with dealers all over the city and wait for them to take the bait before entering the market with your real move in the form of massive orders that would catch dealers wrong-footed and looking silly. Similarly, dealers often know the position of their client directly (through the margin deposit) or indirectly (through industry contacts) and actively push the market against them. The street is littered with stories of one party pulling the wool over the eyes of the other in what seems like an endless game of cat and mouse.

NOT ALL FX DEALERS ARE CREATED THE SAME

Forward/Swap Dealers: The most cerebral of the bunch. More concerned with time than price, these guys have to constantly keep track of value dates and expirations. Calculations can turn complicated in a hurry when clients approach them with obscure set-ups for which they must either quote a price or risk losing a client.

Spot Dealers: Fly-by-the-seat-of-your-pants crowd. Rely more on their gut than their head. Can instantly calculate averages and are above all concerned with their net exposure at any given time. Generally more street-smart than book-smart, they are very attuned to human behavior and trade according to flows. If they smell blood they pounce.

Retail Spot Dealers: Usually ex-bank dealers that were "retired" or decided to move on to a cushier gig. They occupy an awkward place between the interbank and the retail market, with most transactions being generally straight-forward. Cushy job that entails little more than tracking customer flows and offsetting risk with their market makers. Now and then they organize ambushes on their clients, something they revel in. To put it in perspective, the head dealer at one of the major retail FCMs used to show up to work wearing a cap that read "FUCK YOU."

Pretty much sums it up doesn't it?

5
Today's FX Market

The enormous technological advances that we have seen over the last 20 years have had a profound impact on how the FX market operates. Everything from backoffice systems to trading has been affected by the changes, generally making things faster, more accurate, and more reliable. Bank dealers are now less likely to find "surprises" at the end of the day, having second-by-second access to their exposure. Technology has also enabled a new breed of competition to arise for the old-school voice brokers, namely electronic platforms like Reuters, FXAll, EBS, Currenex, etc.

Whereas before a trader was forced to make the rounds in an effort to find a price, he can now instantly see the best tradable bid/ask with a single key stroke. With all of the liquidity providers now imputing their best price into a common platform, it should in theory be a much better way of going about things, and for the most part it is. However, don't feel too sorry for the dealer, for there will always be a place for his trade. Although electronic platforms are great for "vanilla" transactions, if you are a fund trying to push through a large Mexican peso trade in early Sydney time, your only hope for success is contacting a good dealer that can make it happen. No e-platform will ever make a market out of thin air.

A QUESTION OF NUMBERS

Technological advances have helped drive the growth in FX turnover, and although much is said of the tremendous volumes traded on a daily basis, the oft-quoted statistics should be taken with a grain of salt. The FX market is by far the largest and most liquid market in the world, with daily FX turnover estimated at around $2 *trillion*. If this seems like a lot to you, it is because it is. Compare FX volumes to the tiny $50 billion traded at the NYSE or the $800 billion traded in government debt and you get an idea of the size of the market, yet the first thing to take into consideration when hearing that "FX turnover has increased 50% over the last 3 years" is that turnover is measured in US dollars. A depreciating dollar will directly translate into ballooning turnover volume.[1] However, even if the figures are somewhat skewed, the fact remains that billions and billions are being traded every day. So the question becomes, "Who is trading all of these thousands of billions of dollars?"

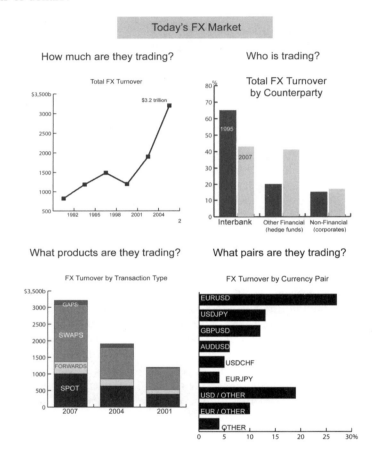

International commerce may at first seem like the obvious answer, yet with the global economy estimated at 40 trillion dollars a year, in theory all of the commercial transactions and corporate hedging would be taken care of in a mere 20 days of trading! The next obvious candidate would have to be hedge fund money, since nowadays everything is blamed on hedge funds. However, since the hedge

---

[1] At constant exchange rates, the turnover increase is around 35 %.
[2] BIS Triennial Survey 2007. Visit www.bis.org for the full report.

fund money allocated to FX is estimated to be around 1 trillion, even leveraging this amount aggressively would still leave a gigantic gap in reporting. So who is doing all the trading?

Where are they trading?

COUNTRY	SHARE
UNITED KINGDOM	34 %
UNITED STATES	17 %
JAPAN	6 %
SINGAPORE	6 %
SWITZERLAND	6 %
HONG KONG	4 %
AUSTRALIA	4 %
GERMANY	3 %

How are they trading?

Average Daily Volume by Dealing Channel

Interdealer Direct 10 %
Voice Brokers 14%
Customer Direct 30%
E-Trading Systems 19%
E-Broking Systems 27%

The truth is that nobody really knows, but it may be the case that turnover numbers are greatly exaggerated due to the multiplying effect of FX transactions and the use of notional funds. For example, when multinational X approaches their bank to trade 100 million euros for dollars, a two-way transaction takes place, so the €100 million goes on both of their books. The bank then quickly contacts one of their counterparties to offset their exposure, which may in turn offset their exposure through the derivatives market. A single transaction can therefore set in motion a whole set of subsequent transactions totaling well over the original €100 million in cash.

Although it is hard to tell exactly where these flows are coming from, what is undeniably true is that FX volumes have been steadily increasing. Volumes are in fact rising at such a tremendous pace that only a fundamental shift in people's perception of FX can explain the current situation.

THE NEW ASSET CLASS

As little as ten years ago, most asset managers regarded FX as an annoying side transaction that simply *had* to be done, and most did not particularly care for it. If a large international mutual fund wanted to buy European stocks, they would simply approach their custodian bank and tell them to take care of it. This was a case of the simpler the better, since in their minds their core competencies lay in picking stocks, not the direction of the dollar. This may seem like a reasonable approach when things are going well, but in times of uncertainty and low yields, every penny begins to matter.

After the bursting of the stock market bubble and 11 September, times got tougher for asset managers and they soon began to look at FX with kinder eyes. They realized that their FX holdings could actually be regarded as a separate asset class, which had to be "optimized" in their constant search for alpha (excess return).

This change in perception proved to be a radical shift for the investment community, and continues to be a major driving force in the FX markets today. More and more funds are now actively managing their FX exposure, either in-house or by employing a currency overlay manager (COM). This renewed the focus on FX and the search for yield has in turn led to the resurgence of the carry trade,[3] which in turn often leaves strong trends in its wake. In an age of low yields and increasingly competitive (efficient) markets, this new brand of FX participant is here to stay.

Black Wednesday, 1992

Perhaps the most infamous FX trade was George Soros & Co's short sterling bet that managed to "break the Bank of England." By September of 1992, Soros and other speculators had begun to take increasingly large short sterling positions on the grounds that the UK economy was suffering from high inflation and a slumping housing market. At the time, the UK had entered the ERM (forerunner to the Euro) at 2.95 Deutsche Marks to the pound, and the GBP/DM pair was allowed to trade a narrow range, with 2.778 set as the bottom. If the rate fell below that level, the Bank of England would have to intervene in order to prop up their currency. On Sep.13th, now known as "Black Wednesday" several big players including Soros and Goldman Sachs realized that the BoE would not be able to support the pound indefinitely, so they decided to stage a massive speculative attack on the currency. The UK Chancellor tried to stir up some demand for the pound by raising rates not once, but *twice* in the same day, yet by evening it became obvious that they could not continue to prop up "Her Majesty" so they decided to throw in the towel and unceremoniously withdrew from the ERM. The pound was then free to trade outside of the fixed range and eventually fell to as low as 2.20 DM. The UK government is said to have lost around 3 billion pounds in their effort to prop up their currency, while Soros is said to have personally taken home around $1 billion in the process......not winning him many friends in the UK!

Moral of the story: When everything is in your favor, go for the home-run trade.

---

[3]Borrowing a low-yielding instrument and trading it for a higher yielding one in an effort to make money from the yield difference. For example, you take a loan from the bank at 5 % and buy bonds yielding 7 %, in effect keeping the 2 % difference.

6
The Players

Since FX prices are shaped by customer flows, in order to fully understand what makes the market tick we need to understand the players involved and their motivations. Although over half of all FX turnover is handled by the interbank market (essentially banks trading with each other) this percentage has been rapidly shrinking (it accounted for two-thirds of all trading 10 years ago) due to the increased participation of sophisticated and varied investors. Where FX was once solely the domain of global banks, nowadays a growing number of speculators such as hedge funds and CTAs actively jostle for space alongside the more traditional players.

In a way, it seems only fitting that the largest market in the world should also have the most varied group of participants, and everybody from the hedge fund crowd to the frequent flier crowd now has an interest in foreign exchange rates. In order to simplify things, we can divide the FX market into the four major types of participants: marker makers, corporate accounts, speculators, and central banks.

MARKET MAKERS (Dealers)

In contrast to the other FX participants, market makers are the only noncustomers in the market and are there instead to provide a service to paying clients. Banks are the only ones with deep-enough pockets to handle the biggest of FX transactions, from billion dollar M&A flows to structured products for corporate clients, but since not everyone can trade directly with a bank specialist brokerage houses have long existed to handle the "leftovers". Unlike bank dealers, whose primary purpose is to make markets for their corporate client base, a dealer for an FX brokerage should play a blind third-party role by simply matching up the orders of their wide customer base and collecting a spread for their trouble (much like a specialist on the NYSE). Speculators can use them to gain anonymity while trading, prop desks may use them for arbitrage, and individuals may use them because of their smaller size.

Although a dealer's role in the market should theoretically be limited to providing liquidity for their clients, in reality much more is expected of a good dealer, and an FX desk is expected to generate substantial "off-the-books" profits for the company by actively trading against their client base.

CORPORATES

Multinationals are the bread-and-butter of the FX world and are, by and large, seen as the most logical participants in the foreign exchange market. Along with insurance and pension funds, they are known as "real money" accounts as opposed to the leveraged crowd, which borrows substantial amounts to trade. The Coca-Colas and GEs of the world receive and make payments all over the world, which necessitates their involvement in the foreign exchange market. These corporate flows need to be carefully predicted and hedged in advance so that accurate budgets and projections may be created. Since corporate clients are not a particularly speculative bunch, they are primarily interested in hedging flows through the forward market. For them, the less volatility, the better.

A well-run and pro-active treasury can have a tremendous impact on a company's bottom line, as in the case of BMW, which successfully avoided being hurt by a 13 % rise in the value of the euro against the dollar in 2003 – unlike rival Volkswagen, which had to take a €400 million hit because of bad hedging decisions.

SPECULATORS (Hedge Funds, CTAs, Prop Desks, COMs)

Speculative traders come in all shapes and sizes and tend to be the most interesting bunch in the FX world. Their primary aim is to generate profits through their views on the market, as opposed to simply collecting transaction fees (brokers) or using FX as a means to an end (corporates). The big players in this group include prop desks (banks trading their own proprietary accounts), hedge funds, commodity trading advisors (CTAs), and currency overlay managers (COMs). These traders have an appetite for risk and a put-your-money-where-your-mouth-is mentality, but their use of leverage also means that they are more prone to "blowing-up" than other participants. Along with dealers, they are responsible for the majority of intra-day moves.

CENTRAL BANKS

The central banks of the world act as the administrators of the FX market. Each national bank is responsible for their currency, and it is no secret that they often play active roles "nudging" the market in their preferred direction. Central banks are loathe to see their currency being used for speculation, and although their primary aim in the FX world is to reduce harmful volatility, if fundamental imbalances exist they will sooner or later be reflected in the exchange rate. Since CBs love to see speculators get hurt, interventions in the market are made at strategic moments to catch the market off-guard, and smaller countries may choose to close the doors to speculators altogether by limiting capital flows.

THE FOOD CHAIN

FX participants are arranged in a certain pecking order that ensures that the top rung always feeds on the bottom dwellers. In this world, the bottom rung of the food pyramid is occupied by the "public", usually customers whose field of expertise lies outside trading currencies (corporates) or unsophisticated market participants (retail). Since everybody feeds off the public (especially banks and brokers) this is not where you want to be, and if you are a retail trader paying a 5 pip spread for a 20 pip trade then you immediately fall into this category.

Hedge funds and other sophisticated speculators, on the other hand, are at the top of this food chain. Due to their speed and market insights, these advanced players are able to prey on banks and brokers that are more concerned with collecting spreads than identifying arbitrage opportunities. It's a speculator's duty to take some of the bank's risk-free profits and pocket them for themselves.

Because a player's positioning on the food chain is dictated by their level of information and speed, retail investors unfortunately often have a hard time overcoming the disadvantages that keep them at the level of the "public".

THE ROLE OF THE SMALL SPECULATOR

Small speculators occupy a very peculiar position in the FX world, and often find themselves at the bottom of the food pyramid being preyed upon by more experienced players. Although the odds are stacked against them, some retail traders do, however, manage to overcome the odds with a mix of confidence and skill that any bank trader would envy. Such is the story of Yukiko Ikebe, a 59-year-old housewife in Tokyo who was recently indicted for evading income taxes from her

roughly 400 million yen trading profits, a story that inspired the head of foreign
exchange at Société Générale in Tokyo to proclaim: "She must have made more
than us! Find her and hire her!" These outstanding individuals have learned not
to "fight" the market, because the market is certainly not fighting them, so they
instead focus their attention on taking whatever the market is willing to give them,
and going by Mrs Ikebe's example it is apparently quite a lot!

Unfortunately these bright stars seem to be few and far between, since the vast
majority of retail spot FX traders are just not very good in the long run. After all, if
market makers profit by trading against their client base, then their client base must
be wrong most of the time for them to make money. Retail traders in any market
make great contrarian indicators, and their positioning is in fact a valued commodity
that is actively traded upon by many funds and money managers. Although you
may think their chances of success are 50/50, somehow amateur traders have the
innate ability to pick tops and bottoms and consistently get chewed up by the
market because of their misguided trading decisions and lax money management
rules (see below).

Retail positioning data provide a great contrarian indicator.

This chart illustrates some of the erroneous logic that is habitually exhibited by the retail crowd and exploited by professionals. Creative Technologies (CREAF) is the maker of the "Zen" mp3 player, commonly seen as the biggest competitor to the iPod. Of course, being number two does not count for much in a market dominated by Apple, and the stock price has reflected this sentiment by trending lower for much of the year. One day in late August, however, Creative announced after the bell that it had won a patent-infringement lawsuit against Apple and that it would receive a one-off payment of $100 million in the settlement.

On the back of the great news, Creative's stock gapped higher the next day and traded as high as 7.60, having closed around 6.00 the previous day. The volume traded was almost ten times the daily average, indicating large retail participation. Dealers were well aware of the news, but maybe surprisingly they begin to sell soon after the opening bell (they were selling while the masses were buying). Why did they choose to go against the tide? If you look at the bigger picture you soon realize that although $100 million may be a nice chunk of change, it will in no way alter the prevailing trend – i.e. the iPod will continue to dominate the market. If the lawsuit had changed the fundamentals of the industry (forcing Apple to stop producing their product, for example) then their reaction would probably have been different, but in this scenario they were happy to sell all day long to the unsuspecting buyers and finish the day with a healthy profit when the buying subsides and the price returns to its pre-news level.

Dealers in any market know how to make money off retail traders.

(c) 2006 Yahoo! Inc.

The trend is obvious, and the market has clearly decided that Apple has brighter prospects.

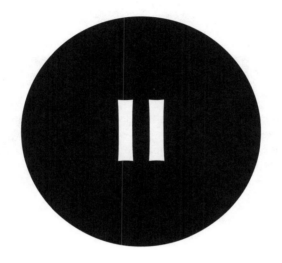

THE RETAIL SIDE
OF THINGS

"A broker will only make you broker"

<blockquote>
Wall Street saying
</blockquote>

Retail FX is not interbank FX, no matter what any broker may want you to believe. The prices are not interbank, the size is not interbank, the counterparty is not interbank, and the rules are not interbank. So what exactly about it is interbank?

How a retail FCM's profits are divided

The generous spread paid by retail traders is the bounty divided up by your broker, the manager of your account, and some large banks. Their motivation is obvious, since the more you trade, the more they make. In a scenario like this, who's looking out for your best interests?

7
Card Stacking

Retail participation in the FX market is nothing new. Before the advent of the euro, Europeans were accustomed to dealing with foreign exchange all the time, and anyone who has lived in a country with a volatile currency will tell you that they always like to keep one eye on the exchange rate. In the UK, spread-betting shops have long offered "punters" the chance to bet on exchange rates[1] and in Asia "Japanese housewives" and their $10 billion of daily trading have been the bane of market professionals for some time, yet the real explosion in on-line currency trading that we have seen in the last five years can be directly attributed to the deregulation in US markets.

Throughout the 1990s, US futures exchanges complained to the government that they were drowning under a mountain of red-tape and outdated reporting measures, which increased their transaction costs and stifled their growth. In order to help the exchanges streamline their operations, the CFTC[2] passed the Commodity Exchange Act and Commodity Futures Modernization Act (CFMA). Under the CFMA, over-the-counter markets were kept exempt from US government oversight and some of the more restrictive regulations on futures exchanges were removed to ensure their global competitiveness. This, combined with the internet revolution, opened the doors for FX brokers (also called FCMs) to target a retail audience and begin offering on-line margin trading accounts. Retail FX brokers thus gained legitimacy by placing the "regulated by the NFA" logo on their website, and the power of the internet meant that these start-ups needed little more than a Reuters line and a toll-free number in order to compete with traditional brokerage houses.

The early years of the retail FX market featured a number of rag-tag outfits consisting of over-caffeinated dealers in tiny Manhattan offices offering their clients spreads wide enough to drive a truck through, and most would surely have continued to live an uneventful life had it not been for the collapse of the internet bubble.

---

[1]Fittingly, these operations fall under the umbrella of the UK's gambling laws.
[2]Commodity Futures Trading Commission.

With the burst of the bubble, FX brokers now had what they had been lacking all this time: a client base in love with day trading that was dying to try something different. The three or four firms that recognized this opportunity and focused all of their attention on their marketing efforts quickly became the market leaders and have never looked back.

These retail operations that have mushroomed in the last five years sit in a still-to-be-defined gray area within the FX market. In theory they should act as little more than middlemen between the true interbank market and their retail client base, but unfortunately because of the nature of the FX market and the lack of regulation some of these outfits bring to mind the unscrupulous "bucket shops" that operated in the early part of the 20th century.

In a time when stock market euphoria was gripping the nation, the typical bucket shop of the 1920s catered to the small investor with big dreams but little market experience. All of the transactions they handled were off-exchange (with the firm taking the other side of all trades), and in order to increase speed customer orders were simply taken at the counter[3] and dumped into a "bucket", to be matched and filled at a later point. Because the orders where not immediately offset in the market, the shops could either wait until the price moved in their favor before filling them (keeping the difference) or wait until the end of the day to match buys and sells at their own "adjusted" price. The dealers that ran the shops knew that in a time of delayed quotes and nontransparent pricing, clients had little way of knowing where the market stood at the exact moment they placed their orders, and thus they would likely be satisfied as long as their orders were filled within the high/low of the day. Because of these advantages, bucket shop operators found it relatively easy to shade prices and take large chunks from both the buyers and the sellers.

Unfortunately, today's retail FX brokers share many traits with these outlawed operations, including:

Nontransparent pricing. The FX market is an over-the-counter market, meaning the price your broker gives you is the price you get. You have no choice in the matter. Pricing is not done through a central exchange, so it may be difficult for the trader to determine if their broker is quoting them "fair" prices or if they are shading the price in their favor.

Encouraging overleveraging. Like the bucket shops, retail FX brokerage firms prey on the small, unsophisticated investor. By extolling the virtues of 200-1 leverage, traders are encouraged to overexpose themselves and be quickly wiped out by small price moves.

Trading against your clients. It is standard practice in the FX world to trade against your client base. Retail trade sizes are too small to be immediately offset in

---

[3] Hence the term over-the-counter (OTC) for nonexchange transactions.

the interbank market, so your broker is forced to take the opposite side of the trade, at least temporarily. The broker may then wait until the client flow is sufficient to offset with their market maker or they may choose to hold the position and effectively trade against their clients. A "no dealing desk" policy simply means that dealers have been replaced with machines, but the fact that they trade against you remains.

> ## Order book information typically available to your market maker:
>
> Real-time summary of client positions.
> Average cost of open positions
> Size and P/L of all open trades
> Outstanding orders
> Location and size of stops
> Flow information
> (who has been buying what/where)
> Real-time positioning of large clients
>
> This information is actively traded upon and often shared with 'preferred' clients/partners.
>
> Ask your broker why all clients aren't given access to this information..

Unfair practices. Although the odds were stacked against the bucket shop client, smart traders could, and did, make money from them. Jesse Livermore,[4] for example, became so good at picking stocks that he was soon banned from all the bucket shops in the East Coast. Casinos do not like winners and neither do FX brokers. A casino may send a crooked dealer to stop the winner's streak and retail FX firms may resort to denying service or complicating execution to such a degree that it makes trading impossible. If anything, this should be a clear sign that your broker is trading against you, since it becomes evident that your broker is losing money if you are posting profits.

The question that comes to mind is, "Why would brokers behave in this manner? Isn't it in their interest to see traders prosper and have them as long-term clients?"

---

[4]Commonly known as the "greatest trader of all time" for his tape-reading ability and his correct timing of the stock market crash of 1929. After a series of ups and downs Livermore ended up taking his own life in a NYC hotel room in 1940, helping solidify the notion that great traders often make for miserable individuals.

The simple answer is "no". Since statistics show that most traders blow-up their accounts before reaching their first anniversary, it is in a broker's best interest to get as much as they can as quickly as they can. There is no such thing as a "long-term" relationship between a market maker and his clients, and while the degree of dodgyness may vary from shop to shop, the capital markets were founded on greed, not charity. Stories of big investment banks ripping off large corporate clients routinely make the news, so is it really any surprise to hear that retail traders do not fare any better? Since dealers routinely change jobs and live on a day-to-day basis (or bonus-to-bonus, actually) it should come as no surprise to learn that they focus purely on short-term profits. A trade is a trade and a deal is a deal, so do not expect any sympathy from your broker/dealer anytime soon. After all, he is not exactly selling ladies shoes, either. A dealer's job is a risky one, and he knows that if you could, you would probably rip him off in a second, so why should he treat you any differently? Although I am sure squeaky-clean shops exist somewhere, I have yet to come across any.

MARKETING MACHINES

Traders have to realize that behind all of the smoke and mirrors retail FX brokers are, above all, marketing machines. The more accounts they open, the more money they make. Because the average survival rate for traders is so low, in order to survive they need a constant flow of new or returning clients, and although some brokers may claim to have over "50K+ clients" in reality the vast majority of those accounts have been dead for quite some time. The actual figure is probably closer to a 10 % retention rate, and even the people running the trading houses have no problems discussing the dreadful odds their clients face. According to Drew Niv, chief executive of FXCM, "If 15 % of day traders are profitable, I'd be surprised."[5]

To secure this constant flow of clients, brokers spend vast amounts of money on marketing schemes that I am sure you have been the target of in the past. They will try everything from huge internet advertising campaigns to direct mail offerings, even going as far as holding trading "conferences" or "seminars". In the end, you can rest assured that they want a return on their investment: your money.

Take, for example, their much-hyped "forex trading contests" that promise to reward the best traders with monthly cash prizes. What could possibly be wrong with rewarding good traders? A lot, actually. Trading contests and dreams of a large payoff place people in direct competition with each other, which, as you may know, tends to only encourage risk taking and lead to terrible money management decisions. If you are trading to beat your neighbor, not simply to make money for your own account, then you can rest assured that you (and your neighbor) will soon find yourself broke. Even if we manage to put aside the ethical dilemma these contests

---

[5]Currency Markets Draw Speculation, Fraud. *Wall St Journal*, 26 July 2005.

bring up and focus squarely on the dollars and cents, we still find brokers coming out on top even when they are the ones paying out to traders on a monthly basis.

Layers between the retail trader and the interbank market

Each layer represents an extra cost. The more layers between you and the market, the higher the costs.

Going by the figures posted by one prominent broker in their "mini" trading contest, four hundred participants with a minimum of $500 in their accounts were involved in the monthly trading contest, which gave out cash prizes to the top three performers ($2500, $1000, and $500) as measured on a monthly percentage return basis. Out of the four hundred accounts, the top three winners all recorded monthly returns in excess of 200 %. Most probably these guys simply leveraged their accounts to the max, picked a volatile pair, closed their eyes, and bought. Not much skill was involved in that brilliant strategy. The really interesting part comes when we shift the attention away from the winners and focus instead on the results of the rest of the field. Out of four hundred participants, less than 150 finished the month above breakeven (a surprisingly high number, actually), and the rest finished with a losing record. Of those with losing records, 55 recorded losses in excess of 95 %; in other words, their accounts were completely wiped out. Now if we compare the payout the broker made to winners ($4000) versus the accounts that were blown-up (at least $27 000) you quickly get an idea of who exactly the winners in this game are. This type of game where lots of small accounts vie for a big payoff is not new; it is usually just called a lottery.

In this sense, forex brokers are simply great at twisting the truth and transforming the laughable into something deemed valuable by traders. Such is the case with their now-popular "hedging" capability. Who else could convince traders that paying twice the spread simply to be flat is actually of benefit to them? These guys should run for Congress!

PRICING

Since retail FX brokers do not have to offset client transactions in an exchange, pricing decisions become critical. Large retail FCMs have their own market makers, a Citi or Goldman for example, which offer them a 1 pip spread or less on the most liquid pairs, which they use as their indicative price. To this rate, they add their 2 or 3 pips (or more!), which is the rate clients see in their trading platforms, which enables them to capture a nice 3 or 4 pip risk-free profit on a round-trip trade – not bad for simply acting as the middle man between the FX "wholesalers" and the retail buyer.

However, because these middlemen are free to manipulate their price feed, they can essentially show their clients any price they want, and the same person that is doing the buying and the selling also becomes the person that controls the prices. If this smells fishy to you, it should; after all, it is the primary reason why exchanges were created in the first place, since the lack of transparency always plays into a dealer's hands.

Price shading occurs when a broker either deliberately stalls their price or shows slightly higher/lower rates in anticipation of a move. If a broker is convinced that the euro is going higher, for example, he will shade his quotes slightly higher to benefit from the move. This is all fairly common practice in the FX world, yet even more appalling manipulation takes place when brokers deliberately spike their feed in order to take out customer orders. If a dealer notices that a bunch of good-sized stops have gathered nearby (remember, they know where your stops lie!), he may choose to mount an attack on them with his buddies or momentarily spike his price feed just enough to take them out.

Naturally, the move will be seen as single blip, not enough to be traded on, but enough to trip the client stops (see below). If a client complains, brokers are shielded by the fact that there is no central exchange from which to compare second-by-second pricing, and are free to offer up any excuse for the move: "There was a large order that pushed through the market" or the classic "Our feeds are faster and reflect true interbank movements." In reality what they are dying to tell you is, "Thanks for noticing; that was a great move! We nailed you!" I'm sure most retail traders have experienced such infuriating behavior, but the nature of the market makes it hard to enforce such downright fraudulent actions.

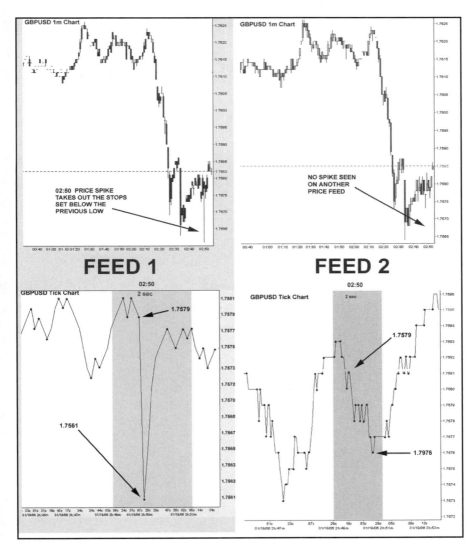

An example of price manipulation. With two feeds from two different FX brokers, you can see how at the same moment one price spikes while the other one does not.

8
Don't Trust Your FCM

As the Chinese general Sun-Tzu once said, "Keep your friends close and your enemies even closer." All traders should heed this advice and keep a watchful eye on their FX broker. These days, dodgy activity seems to be more often the norm than the exception, so it is imperative to conduct your own due diligence on your broker before opening an account. Do not assume that because they proclaim to be large and "well respected" in the industry that that makes them upstanding guys.

According to the NFA, before choosing a broker you should keep some of these things in mind:

You are relying on the dealer's creditworthiness. Basically, if they go down, you go down. Since retail off-exchange forex trades are not guaranteed by a clearing organization, the funds that you have deposited are not insured and do not receive a priority in bankruptcy. Even customer funds deposited by a dealer in an FDIC-insured bank account are not protected if the dealer goes bankrupt (remember REFCO anyone?), so you should first check with the CFTC's website and see the state of their balance sheet.

There is no central marketplace. Unlike regulated futures exchanges (CBOT, CME), in the retail off-exchange forex market there is no central marketplace with many buyers and sellers. The forex dealer determines the execution price, so you are relying on the dealer's integrity for a fair price.

The trading system could break down. If you are using an internet-based electronic system to place trades, some part of the system could fail. In the event of a system failure, it is possible that, for a certain time period, you may not be able to enter new orders, execute existing orders, or modify or cancel orders that were previously entered. A system failure may also result in loss of orders or order priority.

You could be a victim of fraud. As with any investment, you should protect yourself from fraud. Beware of investment schemes that promise significant returns with little risk. You should take a close and cautious look at the investment offer itself and continue to monitor any investment you do make.

At the time of writing, third-party solicitors for retail spot forex trading were still not subject to regulatory oversight, and may make misleading statements and false promises to their heart's content. A Google search on the term "forex" will quickly reveal all kinds of scams and false promises made possible by lax government oversight.

OVERSIGHT

NFA Compliance Rule 2-36(b)(1) states that:

> No Forex Dealer Member or Associate of a Forex Dealer Member engaging in any currency futures or options transactions shall cheat, defraud or deceive, or attempt to cheat, defraud or deceive any person.

However, one quick visit to the NFA, CFTC, or FSA (UK) websites reveals that some of the largest retail FCMs have been reprimanded for things such as:

- Claiming slippage-free execution, guaranteed fills on stop-loss and limit orders and price guarantees on market orders, when in fact the FCM did not provide any of the above.

- In times of volatility, changing the execution trade price post-fact after it had already been confirmed to customers earlier in the day.

- Continuing to advertise "slippage-free" execution even though they knew it was not possible.

- Advertising "commission-free trading", implying that the FCM does not make any money from the transactions.

- Employing nonmember third-party solicitors using misleading promotional materials to solicit customers.

- Claiming that "customer funds are segregated and safe at all times" when in fact they are not.[1]

---

[1] You can check your broker instantly using NFA BASIC (http://www.nfa.futures.org/basic).

Even if they do get caught, most firms are let off with a slap-on-the-wrist fine and never have to admit any guilt. The problem is that although it is a valuable institution, in the end the National Futures Association is a self-regulatory agency, and asking forex brokers to "self-regulate" themselves is like asking athletes to self-regulate themselves for steroid abuse. It is just not very effective.

The Commodity and Futures Trading Commission, on the other hand, is the government-sponsored body that oversees all exchange-related activity in the US (FSA in the UK). These are the guys that send crooked dealers and ponzi schemes to jail, but their FX oversight is limited because of the spot market's over-the-counter nature. The CFTC is set up to regulate exchange-traded markets, so in FX they can do little more than enforce outright scams and fraud.

The one way that the CFTC and NFA have found to effectively push the smaller FCMs out of the market is by enforcing the minimum net capital requirements, which up until recently have been little more than a joke. Because the rise of the retail forex market caught regulators sleeping, loopholes in outdated 30-year-old minimum funding regulation enabled new FX brokers to establish themselves with little, if any, capital. These fly-by-night outfits (often companies repeatedly created, and closed, by the same individuals) were opened with as little as $250 000 in capital, and could therefore not withstand even the smallest adverse turn of events before going under. Although this should have scared the daylights out of their retail clients with millions of dollars in nonsegregated trading accounts, most of the time they were blissfully unaware of the consequences (until it was too late) due to a lack of awareness programs. The subsequent bankruptcy of several small brokers (that took their client's money with them) finally led the government to raise the minimum net capital requirement and begin to crack down on these woefully underfinanced operations.

As of now, the minimum net capital requirements have been raised to several million dollars (see Notes section for the full regulation) and the once-nonexistent audits have been stepped up dramatically. A futures commission merchant who is not in compliance with these requirements has ten business days to achieve compliance or immediately cease doing business and go into liquidation, which still leaves retail clients out in the cold. Slowly but surely this has begun to weed out most of the dangerously under-funded brokers, yet many more "borderline" brokers still remain. The only way to ensure the safety of your funds is to only trade with brokers who are well above their minimum capital requirements. FCMs are required to file monthly reports with the CFTC stating their current finances, but remember that since these reports are only audited once a year you are for the most part relying on your broker's word.[2]

---

[2] A full version is available online: http://www.cftc.gov/marketreports/financialdataforfcms/index.htm.

As of 31 May 2007, this was how the major FX brokers stood:

In good standing	Borderline
FXCM $51 000 000	Money Garden (MG) $3 399 844
GFT $48 000 000	Forex Club $3 304 000
Oanda $44 000 000	MB Futures $3 080 000
FX Solutions $20 000 000	GFS Futures & Forex $3 074 000
Gain Capital $20 000 000	Nations Investments $1 699 000
CMS $10 000 000	Velocity4X $1 587 000
	SNC Investments $1 565 000
	Direct Forex LLC $1 523 000
	FiniFX $1 464 000
	One World Capital $1 105 000
	Royal Forex Trading $1 102 000
	FXDD $781 000

The bottom line is that today's retail spot FX market is the Wild West of the investment world, where virtually anything goes. Government oversight of such a complex and fundamentally OTC market is very hard to implement, but if the shoddy dealings continue then look for much tighter regulations to be implemented down the line, although the retail FX brokers will surely not go down without a fight. In fact, FX brokers are raking in so much money these days (hundreds of millions of dollars) that they have even hired their own lobbyists to keep government at bay. You know you have hit the big time when you can afford to buy a lobby!

DEMAND CHANGE

For the retail trader to get a fair shake, the deceptive dealings (long outlawed in most other markets) must simply come to an end. How can the FX brokers defend their actions (some of which call for jail time in other markets) and continue to tell the general public that intra-day FX trading is a great "investment" and deeming it "easy"? How can they continue to do business with people that solicit clients through false marketing and fraudulent claims?

New regulation needs to be put into place that will guarantee transparency in pricing and safety of funds to the retail client, but it is up to the average trader to plant the seeds of change by complaining vigorously to the government authorities at the slightest hint of dishonorable dealings. We will all be in a better place once a fair set of rules are adopted that lets both brokers and traders flourish. After all, fair dealings should be every broker's duty, not choice.

9
Third-Party Services

The retail FX market's rise in popularity has created a whole new side-industry focused on providing a range of services geared toward the retail trader. Hundreds of companies now offer clients great money-making trading signals or programs, and hitherto unknown market participants have now suddenly become recognized market "experts" eager to dispel their boundless wisdom to traders (for a fee, of course). Needless to say, the actual services they provide leave much to be desired.

Let me put it this way: if you had a proven, money-making FX trading system would you sell it to the general public? If you had a proven system that accurately predicted winning lottery numbers, would you sell it for $50 a pop? Probably not. Hedge funds and private traders spend millions of dollars developing and safeguarding their trading systems, but you can still find hundreds of different trading programs for sale on the internet or trading magazines. Common sense tells us that these "systems" are probably not very good to begin with.

When looking at third-party providers, it is good to be more than a bit skeptical of their services. For example, if the "guru" you are looking at does not trade his own recommendations, then what is his downside? If the results cannot be verified (note that simply posting them on a website is not verifying them!) then what is the point?

IF THE SUBSCRIPTION IS FREE, HOW DO THEY MAKE MONEY?

To ensure that you are getting a fair shake, it is best to make sure that the "expert" or "system" has no relationship with any broker. A dead giveaway is them asking you to trade with their "preferred" broker, which is just another way of saying that they make a pip or two out of every trade that you place. You want to steer clear of anyone making money from your trading, since at the end of the day they do not care if you win or lose money; they just want you to trade.

Looking around the internet I have also seen many "mentors" popping up, who offer to show traders the ropes in exchange for a fee. Although the practice of mentoring has long been established in the markets, paying someone for this kind of service is simply a bad idea; all you have to do is understand their motivation.

When a new trader joins a firm he will pair up with a more experienced trader who will teach him how to become a great trader. The motivation there is simple: they have a vested interest in seeing their pupils succeed because of the time and money they have invested in them, and the hope is that they make millions for the whole company. Now compare that to mentors offering to teach you for a fee. What is their motivation? To make their pupils succeed or to simply generate fees? If this mentor/trader is so great, why is he teaching random strangers? The truth is that before these guys became popular FX gurus, they were selling miracle brooms on infomercials. In the real world, mentors *choose* their students, not the other way around.

The best mentors you can possibly find are friends or acquaintances whom you know to be good traders, since they have verifiable results and their motivation is clear.

SCAMS

According to the CFTC, the amount of FX scams has skyrocketed in the last few years. This is a direct result of the increase in popularity of forex trading and the lax oversight by government agencies. A quick web search is enough to show the full range of forex scams out there, some promising 1000 % return with no risk! Before entering into any investment scheme, every investor should regularly check the CFTC's website and also make a point to regularly check www.futuresbuzz.com for the latest industry news and FX scams.

THE GOOD GUYS

Therefore, if looking for a second opinion, who do you trust? There are many great analysts and third-party services out there; you just have to make sure you pick the right ones. A whole community of professional technicians, economists, and analysts exists to service the institutional trading industry, providing innovative trading ideas or market advice. The difference is that they make their money through their calls (reputation) not through your trading (by getting referral money from the broker). I have personally used several subscription services in the past, with varying results, but have noticed that good services have a few things in common:

- **First, they are not cheap.** As the saying goes, you get what you pay for.

- **Second, they have a track record.** Not just a cool website.

- **Third, they have real-world FX trading experience.** They can be ex-prop traders, dealers, treasurers, etc. Basically they know how the real FX world works, and take into account the manipulation, aberrations, and "irrationality" that sometimes prevails in these markets.

- **Fourth, there is a time and money-management aspect to their analysis.** It is useless to tell the average trader that the euro will drop to 1.20 if first they have to go through 300 pip gyrations and wait for three months. Opportunity cost is a real cost for most traders with limited liquidity. The last thing you want to do is have your equity locked in a trade that is not moving while bypassing other (maybe better) trading opportunities.

The bottom line is that every great trader has paid their "tuition" to the market, usually in the way of years and thousands of dollars. Don't expect much from a $19.99 system. Success is the direct product of hard work and determination, and you have to learn to trust your own analysis and trading skills. Remember that self-confidence is a hallmark of all great traders.

RULE 1. Never take the advice of someone who is not willing to put money behind their so-called analysis. If they are not willing to take a hit, then what is their downside to making a prediction?

RULE 2. Never listen to anyone "talking their book". Most jokers on chat forums are sitting on positions deep underwater and are desperate to get out. Any advice they can possibly give you is losing advice and should be used as a contrarian indicator if anything. Even the big names routinely talk their book. When Bill Gross of PIMCO (biggest bond trader in the world) appears on CNBC to give his views on the market, do you really think he is going to say something that goes against his positions?

10
Fighting Back

If you are feeling discouraged having realized just how far the odds have been stacked against the individual trader, rest assured that there are a few simple measures that can be immediately implemented to gain back some of the lost ground. The brokers may have initially gained the upper hand, but they have by no means left the retail trader without recourse.

USE DIFFERENT PRICE FEEDS

If you use the same price feed on your trading platform and your charting applications, then you are essentially trading with blinkers on. By limiting yourself to your FCM's artificially created bubble, you are giving up the power to become judge and executioner. Your stops may be run or you may trade off manipulated prices, but you would never realize that the moves did not correspond to the general market.

As a trader, you want to remain at all times objective and have as broad a view as possible of the market, something that cannot be accomplished using a single feed. Having a second or third feed is your way of getting a "second opinion" on the market and gives you a way to confirm the price action. Your platform feed should only be used for placing trades, but your strategy and analysis should rely on the purest, most unbiased price feed you can find. Most retail traders do not have the luxury of trading with a Reuters or EBS feed, but rest assured that alternative sources can be found. Every trader should spend some time comparing different feeds and charts to see how they perform in fast-moving markets when retail platforms regularly freeze their prices (and notice that demo feeds are different from live feeds). Having a stable and faithful charting application is especially vital to all short-term traders.

Do a search for yourself and find one that suits your needs, but remember that most of these "informative" websites are actually run or sponsored by brokers, so make sure that you know where the price feed is coming from. It may be worth the added cost of subscribing to an independent and dedicated charting package, since the benefit of receiving an accurate picture of the market will more than offset the cost in the long run. Before choosing one, however, ask them who provides them with their streaming FX data feed.

KEEP DETAILED RECORDS

The next thing that traders can do to gain back some of the lost ground is to keep detailed trading records. The number one reason is that most slighted traders find it difficult to take action against their broker owing to lack of evidence. Clients may feel cheated when their orders are not filled correctly, orders disappear from their screen, or when they find open trades suddenly closed, but it is all very difficult to prove. When you call your broker to complain you may state that "my order disappeared!", to which they may reply "do you have proof?" This often turns the matter into a your-word versus their-word scenario, which is why it becomes imperative to keep good trading records.

An easy way to do this is to take screen shots. You can find and download a variety of applications on the web, and taking screen shots of your orders in the market, trades, or any other important market activity (like unlawful price spikes) gives you a solid foundation on which to argue any future disagreement. Professionals do it and so should you.

OFFICIAL ACTIONS

If you feel you have been wronged and cannot come to a suitable agreement with your broker, do not hesitate to contact either the CFTC or the NFA. Although most brokers will usually fold when threatened with official action, if they instead choose to call your bluff go directly to these agencies since both offer programs that may help clients resolve disputes with brokers. You do not need to hire a lawyer to file a complaint, and usually taking this initial step is enough to scare a broker into a (reasonable) settlement, since the last thing they want on their official record is another disgruntled trader.

The NFA offers an arbitration program to help customers and NFA Members resolve disputes. Information about NFA's arbitration program is available by calling NFA at 800-621-3570 or visiting the Dispute Resolution section of its web site at www.nfa.futures.org.

Similarly, the CFTC offers a reparation program for resolving disputes. If you want information about filing a CFTC reparations complaint, contact the CFTC's Office of Proceedings at 202-418-5250 or visit the CFTC's website at www.cftc.gov.

In addition, if you suspect any wrongdoing or improper conduct by your FCM, you may file a complaint with the NFA and CFTC by telephone or online:

www.nfa.futures.org/basicnet/complaint.aspx
www.cftc.gov/enf/enfform.htm

Your broker is banking on the fact that most clients do not go through the hassle of reporting their bad habits, so do everyone a favor and contact the authorities if you suspect suspicious activity. In the end, it is up to traders to monitor and stay on top of all forex brokers.

TRADE WITH THE CME

If you are fed up with your broker's obnoxious habits, an obvious alternative to trading with an off-exchange broker is to trade through an exchange. The Chicago Mercantile Exchange operates its own clearing house and virtually eliminates credit risk by acting as the counterparty to every transaction. An additional benefit to the individual is that your funds are held in segregated accounts, meaning that they are protected in case of bankruptcy (unlike on-line brokers). Hedge funds and individual traders have used the CME for years to transact their FX business, so take a look at their FX offering and see if it is right for you.

OPENING A TRADING ACCOUNT

Make sure to check your broker first. Visit the NFA/CFTC/SFA websites and don't trade with any firms not under their oversight. Better yet, perform your own due diligence and go visit their office!

Don't judge a broker's execution by their demo accounts. Demos are marketing gimmicks meant to lure people into trading. The execution on your demo account will be perfect, unlike when you go "live".

Always remember that the cost of switching is low, but the cost of staying with an unfair broker is huge!

Use your trading platform ONLY to enter and exit positions

Constantly looking at your changing P/L will prove hard on your psyche and makes many traders enter/exit their positions too soon. Professionals don't fix their attention on their P/L, but rather on the price action.

The blinking prices and constant swings in equity are used by brokers to distract the trader and amplify the gambling instinct. Try instead to think of the moves in terms of pips, not dollars and cents.

TRADING HABITS

Of course the number one thing traders can do to shift the odds in their favor is to become better traders. This sounds obvious, but it is true. It is much easier to place the blame on bad dealers, systems providers, etc., than on yourself, and for all of the shoddy dealings a retail trader may receive, at the end of the day it is usually their lack of experience and/or bad trading habits that are responsible for the miserable results.

The learning curve can be steep and uncompromising, and in this market there is no free lunch to be had. All traders, even the most successful ones, have paid their "tuition" to the market and all realize that the key to becoming successful is survival. Simply put, the longer you stay in the market the better your chances are of turning into a great trader. For new traders this means establishing your survivability in the market and for experienced traders it means not falling into bad habits.

Obviously, even with all of the sophisticated charting and analytical software available nowadays success is still extremely difficult to accomplish, and moving up the learning curve can take a degree of dedication, capacity, and motivation that many traders simply do not possess. This leads many retail traders to "outsource" the analytical work to a third party, which can prove extremely hazardous since before you know it you find yourself blindly following the advice of some market guru, expert, or system. If it were only so easy! The actual decision-making process is the hardest part of trading, so make sure that you keep a firm grasp on it.

Once we put aside all of the nonsense handed out by brokers and gurus, it is time to get into the meat of becoming a great FX trader. What exactly does it take to post steady profits in this business? What trading rules do professionals adhere to? What FX tricks exist out there that can help improve your performance?

The second half of this book is intended to give active traders the information and tools they need to survive in the FX market and begin developing their own habits and techniques that will turn them into successful traders.

JOINING THE 10 %

11
Becoming a Great Trader

Anyone who has ever traded knows that it can be an exhausting psychological battle that leaves you mentally and physically spent at the end of the day. Although trading is not easy, many people choose to make it even harder for themselves by simply jumping in without taking a second to understand the different styles and how they relate to their personality. By trading "against the grain", you are setting yourself up for a constant personal psychological battle (should I cut or stay) that often leads to bad decision making, losses, and unhappiness.

Matching up your personality with your trading style helps to minimize these personal battles, and if you are a new trader, the first step should be to figure out what kind of trader you have inside you.

TRADING TO YOUR STRENGTHS

Assuming you think you have the skills and drive needed to become a great trader, figuring out what kind of trader you want to be (more than just a "winning trader"!) is a critical step that requires some personal reflection. Although this does not require you to travel to the Gobi Desert to find yourself, you should spend some time figuring out what trading approach best suits your personality.

For example, if you feel you are patient, methodical, and can generally keep your emotions in check, then you may benefit from trading on a longer time frame approach. Do you prefer to play chess or video games? On the other hand, if you are a high-energy, impatient, and emotional individual, you may choose to trade intra-day for the instant gratification it provides.

The difference between holding longer-term positions and going home every night flat is more than just a technical one, since watching profits fly away during momentary retracements can prove more painful to some than taking small losses intra-day. Needless to say, the best traders are completely detached and have absolutely no problem watching their P/L gyrate, but in reality they are few and far between.

All traders, whether self-taught or not, must at some point ask themselves this question: "Am I improving?" Answering this question honestly will save you a mountain of heartache down the road, since it is of no use to waste valuable time and money doing something that does not fit your skill set. If you feel that you are improving (measured by your P/L), then stick with it. If after several years you do not see any improvement in your trading, then you must have the courage to call it quits. Some people make good architects, some make good traders; it is as simple as that. I cannot make a jump-shot to save my life, so I make no pretension of an NBA career.

If, for whatever reason, you are set on becoming a trader, proper money management is by far the most important factor in achieving success. When you think about it, most traders spend most of their time trying to figure out *when* to trade, instead of *how much* to trade, which is surprising given that money management is the *only* thing a trader can actually control!

There is no guaranteed way to make money (except collecting spreads), and even the best and the brightest are often wrong more than they are right. The market is bigger than you, bigger than me, and definitely smarter than all of us. We are bound to be wrong and make mistakes, but proper money management techniques enable us to weather sustained drawdowns and live to fight another day. Funnily enough, the biggest public misconception about traders is that they regularly take huge risks, when in reality great traders aim to minimize their risk relative to their returns at any given moment.

Whether trading a mechanical system or in a discretionary fashion, all traders should know beforehand how much they are willing to wager. Ask yourself: how do I determine my position size? How do I set my stops? All too often traders choose arbitrary numbers that have little to do with proper money management, and exit according to their "pain threshold" instead. Our innate fear of failure makes us place too much importance on not losing, rather than learning to manage our losses comfortably.

The good thing about money management is that it is easy to implement. Although good trading systems may be impossible to find, good money management rules do exist, and the best way to see if your money management needs tweaking is by looking at your results. For example, if your losers are substantially smaller than your winners, then you may want to consider taking slightly larger positions. If you consistently post large winners and losers, you should consider taking smaller positions to mitigate the risk of ruin. Proper money management maintains the all-important risk – reward balance in check, and although your plans may vary from those I present here, the bottom line of any system should be the same: to minimize the chance of blowing-up. Long-term success in this business is achieved by accumulating steady profits and occasionally hitting the home-run trade, and the longer you stay in the market, the more times you get to swing at the ball.

OVERLEVERAGE

Some years ago, Procter & Gamble blindly entered into a series of leveraged derivative trades and discovered to their great surprise that leverage not only magnifies gains but, more importantly, it also magnifies losses, in their case to the tune of $300 million. This incident brought to life the risks of leverage to the corporate crowd, but retail traders are still all too often unaware of the inherent risks. Leverage, or gearing, is a double-edged sword that should be used sparingly, something not helped by the fact that retail FX brokers constantly extol the virtues of 200-1 leverage. By making it seem that "with $1000 dollars you can control $200 000" is a good thing, they suck naïve traders into the leverage trap, since constantly over-leveraging your trades is the equivalent of always driving at 100 mph . . . sooner or later you are going to crash and burn.

Taking a $1000 starting balance, if you were to trade $200 000 in EURUSD, a mere ten point move (a 0.1 % move) against you would translate into 20 % of your account equity getting wiped out. In fact, just by entering the trade (spread), you would already be down 6 % on the trade, which is much more than any permissible loss. Trading position sizes this big in relation to your account size mean that you are essentially trading yourself into a corner, and any market noise is bound to wipe out your account. The brokers love this, of course, since it means easy money for them. If you are overleveraging your trades, then you may as well be handing over your cash to your broker.

Professional money managers generally use no more than two to five times leverage, and the retail investor should definitely not use more than ten. To put that in perspective, using ten times leverage on a $1000 account means that the price would have to move 1000 points against you before your account is wiped out. That is a lot of room to maneuver, and it gives the trader greater flexibility.

FLEXIBILITY

Choosing the right amount of leverage is the first critical step in maintaining your flexibility in the market, which is critical if you are to survive for the long-haul. Flexibility in trading means giving yourself options: options to enter a trade, to stay in it, and to exit. By becoming overexposed to any one position, you essentially remove options from your table until you are faced with an "all-or-nothing" trade, and in the FX world your survival is measured in days, not years.

Since the currency markets are not one-way streets, the normal gyrations of the market mean that, given time, you will usually have an opportunity to get out of a bad trade or enter a position that you may have missed. Most traders have had the frustrating experience of getting stopped-out, only to see the market return back to your entry at some point later in the day. The only way to get around these sometimes arbitrary market movements is to stay flexible and trade multiple lots.

By trading only one lot you are essentially making a 50/50 bet that the rate will move in your direction. Besides not being very wise (it has a negative expected outcome when you take the spread into consideration), it is also not much fun. You should try to think of your initial entry as your toe testing the temperature of the water in the pool. If you find out it is too cold, then you can sit it out, but if it is just the right temperature, then you are free to jump right in. Trading small until you think you have all of the information and confirmation you need gives you the flexibility to properly position yourself for the move, or pull out with a small loss if your analysis proved incorrect. As you may well know, for some reason the FX gods see fit to test our mettle every time we enter a trade by moving the market immediately against us, but trading multiple lots means that our first entry does not become critical and we give ourselves a cushion while the market decides where it wants to go. Trading in this way also means missing out on far fewer trades when compared to the all-in approach, since pulling the initial trigger becomes rather painless and makes the decision-making process much less stressful.

To properly trade multiple lots you must first calculate the total amount you are willing to risk before you enter your trade. Again, different traders take different risks, but it is safe to say that the intra-day trader should not risk more than 1–2 % of their account size on any one position. This means that for a $10 000 account, your loss should never be greater than $200 *on all lots combined*. Look back on your trading and see how big your losses typically are. If you are an intra-day trader and every time you lose you end up taking a 3–5 % hit, then you need to stop immediately and come up with better money management rules. This is the same type of analysis that professionals regularly run on their trading, and it proves very insightful since the reasons for your underperformance will most often be glaring.

Trading with proper money management rules will not guarantee you success, but it will prevent you from falling into the money trap. The "more I bet, the more I win" mentality is not for traders but for gamblers, and using their logic is a sure road to ruin. Avoiding this trap simply means learning to manage your losses by using simple guidelines:

- Never risk more than 2 % on any one position.
- Never trade more than five times leverage on any one position.
- Trade multiple lots with multiple entries.
- If you cannot afford multiple 100 000 lots, trade mini lots.

If you don't think trading mistakes will happen to you, just take a look at what some "pros" did:

2003: Shares in now-bankrupt internet firm Exodus surged more than 59 000% after a bank trader accidentally bid $100 for shares that were trading around 17 cents at the time!

2002: A colossal blunder by Bear Stearns saw the firm sell $4 billion worth of stock at the closing bell instead of the intended $4 million! Fortunately for the firm, they were only filled on $600m or so of the orders before realizing their goof.

2001: Just before the close of the UK market, a fat-fingered Lehman Bros employee mistakenly sold $500m worth of stock – 100 times the intended amount. The slip-up temporarily dropped the FTSE more than 2%!

2001: An absent-minded UBS trader hoping to sell 16 shares of Japanese company Dentsu at 600 000 yen each mistakenly sold 600 000 shares at 16 yen each! Before he knew it, the trader was already $120m in the hole..

1998: Perhaps the most classic blunder of all time was made by a now-infamous Salomon trader who is said to have accidentally sold £850m worth of French government bonds......simply by leaning on his keyboard!

12
Picking the Right Approach

Although proper money management guidelines are the foundations needed to support any sort of trading strategy, at the core of all trading is the fundamental reasoning, a model or system used by traders to enter and exit positions. Broadly speaking, FX traders can be divided into the fundamentalist and the technical crowd. On the one hand, fundamentalists choose to place their bets based on macroeconomic factors such as interest rates, GDP, inflation, current account imbalances, etc., and their relation to a currency's intrinsic "value". Much like equity managers who like to buy "undervalued" companies, fundamental traders use economic models to forecast theoretical exchange rates and trade deviations from these.

The technical crowd, on the other hand, cares less about the underlying economic picture and instead prefers to rely on two things only: time and price. In their thinking, a currency's past behaviour is the best predictor of future exchange rates, so they focus on identifying purely mathematical reasons for entering/exiting trades, such as buying a currency after it moves $X\%$ in a one direction or using chart patterns to guide their trading.

Although the fundamentalist approach may seem like the more logical way to go, extensive research into the matter actually indicates that technical trading is a much more profitable way to trade FX. Although the "value investor" mindset may pay off in equities, it seems that this line of reasoning is utterly useless in forecasting exchange rates (especially in the short run) because of central bank intervention and other market nuances, and it gets decidedly beaten by using a simple randomizer model. This may explain why economists' forecasts are undeniably horrible, and to the short-term trader it means that they should focus their attention on the technical side of trading, if only for the simple reason that it seems to be more profitable. That being said, technical trading is no sure road to riches either.

USING TECHNICALS

Since the advent of trading, the trading community has been obsessed with ways of predicting or forecasting the future through their use of models. As computational power increased over time, so did the popularity of technical or quantitative trading models and now a wide variety of these are used, ranging from simple moving-average systems to complex neural network algorithms. Unfortunately most, if not all, models have built-in biases, so an unquestioning belief in them is extremely dangerous. To prove this point, a famous study was conducted where thousands of different indicators and technical tools were tested in an effort to find the best forecaster of US GDP growth. After an exhaustive search and countless regressions, one leading indicator was found that seemed to fit the data perfectly: buttermilk production rates in Bangladesh! Yet I still have not figured out how to get that on my Bloomberg.

Most risk models still in use today consider the one-day October 1987 market crash to be a one-in-a-billion event, or the statistical equivalent of getting hit by lightning and being attacked by a shark at the same time. Long Term Capital Management and other seemingly advanced hedge funds were done in by these "sigma-nine" events, something that probabilistically speaking is so unlikely (according to their risk models) that it simply does not happen. If that is the case, then how is it that we keep witnessing these "impossible events" over and over again?[1] It is certainly not due to a lack of intelligence or computing power on their part.

In order to understand better why all probability-driven models have limitations that will eventually lead them to fail spectacularly, it is useful to look at a very simple example. Imagine yourself sitting at a stop waiting for the bus to come. You know the frequency of the bus service (every ten minutes), but not the actual arrival time. If the buses run according to schedule, then the probability of a bus arriving in the first minute of you getting to the stop is one in ten. The longer you wait, the higher the chances of the bus arriving any minute, and if you have been sitting at the stop for nine minutes then you can be pretty sure that the next bus is around the corner (at least that is what the model predicts). More sophisticated models may take into account the average time it takes for a bus to arrive, or externalities such as weather and traffic, but either way the model still essentially says that the more you wait, the higher the probability of the bus arriving. Of course, the average person has enough common sense to begin to distrust the model once fifteen or twenty minutes have passed, and you begin to ask yourself, "Is this bus ever going to come?" Maybe it broke down or had an accident. Rest assured that after a sufficient amount of time has passed, there will be no one left at the bus stop – no

---

[1] Hedge fund managers have long made fun of the quant models, and often joke "This is terrible! Today I just had a loss that's a nine sigma event! That's the third time this year!" (even though it should only happen once in ten thousand years or more).

one except the model, that is. People are smart enough to realize when the rules of the game have changed (the bus schedule becomes useless after a certain amount of time has passed), while probability-driven models never take into account the fact that the model itself may be wrong and thus continue to wait for a bus that may, or may not, come. This critical flaw is essentially what makes model-driven trading approaches blow-up spectacularly, and common sense dictates that the world is simply a lot more complex than any risk-model builder would have you believe.

Technical trading proves especially attractive to retail traders because it offers a way to "make sense" out of a sometimes senseless market, and many find the possibility of discovering the "holy grail" of trading systems simply too good to pass up. Yet those obsessed with trying to find *the* indicator or trading system would be better served in spending that time trying to understand the market instead of trying to outsmart it, since the only money-making machines that I know of are owned by the central banks of the world.

The clear benefit that systematic trading gives us is order. Having a clear, organized, and coherent strategy is fundamental to trading success. Although in the end your "system" may or may not prove to be profitable, you should always have a clear understanding as to *why* you are entering the position, and technicals help us tremendously in this regard. Generally speaking, the simpler the model, the more elegant and useful it becomes, since charts filled with lines, indicators, and all kinds of technical tools only serve to distract the trader away from the crucial price action. At a time when quantitative trading has been finally accepted by the general trading community, the intrinsic virtues of technical analysis are hard to discern since often it is traders' combined actions that turn them into self-fulfilling prophecies. If everyone follows the same indicator, then when it flashes a buy signal everyone will go ahead and buy ... and surprise, the price goes up! A kind of "chicken and egg" scenario has emerged and, more importantly, the retail crowd's love of technical analysis has also turned "obvious" technical levels into a magnet for stop hunters. Many funds (including ours) actively front-run other people's models by anticipating the trading signals their systems will generate and then positioning themselves for the slight pop created by their execution. If anything, you should make a point to stay away from any clear technical levels, since the price action around these are bound to be full of dealer manipulation, which is why it is never wise to trade breakouts in FX. With the amount of price "management" that goes on in the forex world, false breaks are more often the norm than the exception. Chances are that other traders will have also identified the same important support/resistance levels that you did, and set their stops accordingly. Dealers know this, obviously, and routinely go after them, thus creating the false breaks.

Learn to use technical indicators, but also learn when to ignore them. Find something that works for you and stick with it. We know that no strategy is always profitable, so the key for technical traders is to identify and understand your system's strengths and weaknesses. This lets you limit your exposure in traditionally bad times and double-up in the good ones. Does your system work best in high-volatility or slow markets? Does it work best in ranging or trending environments? Does it work best for USD pairs or others? These are the types of questions you should be asking of your system, since just like the blackjack player you want to end up betting only when the odds are in your favor. In isolation all technical tools are essentially the same, and only in their application will you find the true differentiator. This is why I think it is vital to keep a discretionary element to your trading, even if it is simply knowing when to turn your system "on" or "off". We know that the only instrument that can consistently beat the market is the human mind, so make sure to use it.

DISCRETIONARY TRADING

Purely discretionary traders rely on their experience, gut feeling, and reading of the price action to make trading decisions, and for FX traders this means coming to grips with what makes the market tick. Intra-day FX prices are shaped by flows, and as we know these flows may be the speculative bets of a large hedge fund or they may simply be the hedging activity of an exporter. Either way, supply and demand is what sets short-term prices, which is why we say that in FX there is no such thing as a fair price. Even if the macro backdrop favors a dollar decline, a large buy order will disrupt prices in the short run and drive the dollar higher until the demand is satisfied. For the intra-day trader the thinking behind these flows is not important; price is all that matters.

Getting a proper "feel" for the market comes down to understanding the price action. Price action is that magical thing that scares traders out of their positions and lures them into traps. Watching the bids and the offers get hit is the equivalent of the old-time tape reading made famous by Jesse Livermore and other "punters", who used to read the ticker tape attentively in an effort to gauge short-term price trends according to price and volume. Price action reflects the tug-of-war that is constantly going on between the buyers and the sellers in the market, and to the experienced trader it can also be a window into the market's footing.

Since short-term price movements are largely dictated by the maneuvering of the "big boys" in the market, it is in the interest of every small speculator to closely follow the price action in order to find the "footprints" that all large players inevitably leave behind. Needless to say, reading price action is easier in exchange-traded markets, where volume information is available and institutional block orders are more easily detected, but in FX those with no flow information can still glean the market's intentions by looking at the order flow information left behind in the form of chart patterns and noting how prices react near important pivot points. Correctly reading price action is not something that can easily be taught, and over time traders find that it is more of an art form than a science.

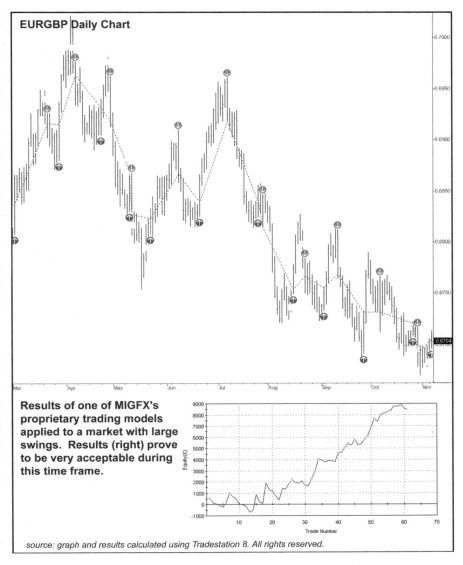

EURGBP Daily Chart

Results of one of MIGFX's proprietary trading models applied to a market with large swings. Results (right) prove to be very acceptable during this time frame.

All mechanical trading systems have built-in biases and flaws that you must be aware of.

One way to properly gauge the state of the market is by studying charts. Charts are so valuable to the intra-day trader because they paint a graphical representation of the price action, and over time telltale patterns emerge that can give us an insight into the market's footing and intention.

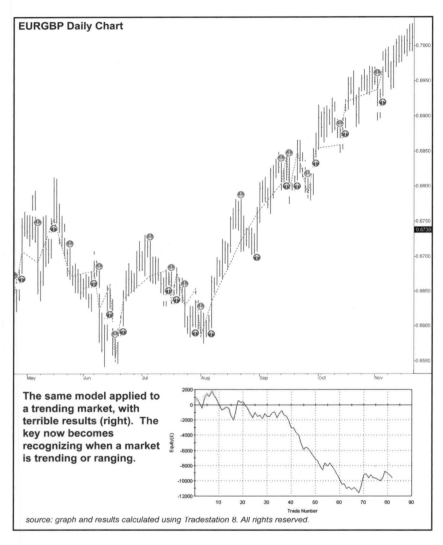

EURGBP Daily Chart

The same model applied to a trending market, with terrible results (right). The key now becomes recognizing when a market is trending or ranging.

Systematic trading systems are all bound to fail systematically sooner or later, which is why keeping a discretionary element is vital.

Familiarity with price action reading is the key to discretionary trading and allows traders to time more accurately their technically or fundamentally inspired entries and exits. The point is not necessarily to trade off the price action directly, but rather to learn to "predict" moves so that you can anticipate the market reaction and plan your response accordingly. With the help of a fast feed traders can learn to interpret the price action by simply looking at the way prices react near important levels.

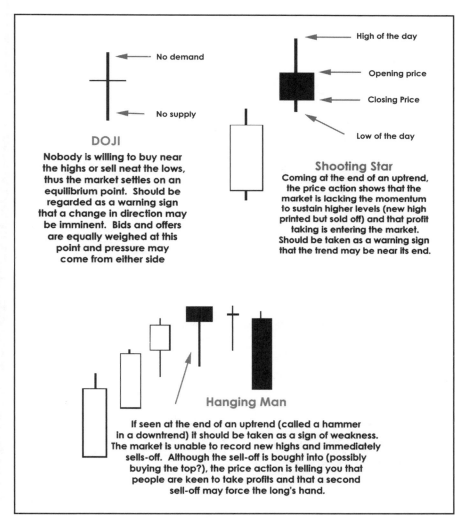

Candlestick reading is a great way to visualize the price action and identify meaningful setups instantly.

For example, if a large option is rumored to lie near a big figure, the price action near the figure will usually let you know exactly what is being protected, and how vigorously. If the pair is sold off as it approaches the big figure but is then quickly bought back 10–20 pips lower, that may be a signal that the option protection guys are re-loading (selling near the figure and then covering their shorts). If this happens several times then you can be pretty certain that they are indeed protecting

Footprints that real-money driven moves leave behind.

Typical speculative price action.

their option, and you should keep an eye on the London or NY options cut after which the selling may disappear and the rate may be free to move higher.[2]

In order to read the price action properly, start by asking yourself these types of questions:

- What does the market do immediately after news is released?
  Initial move higher, followed by a rapid sell-off (dealers are fading the move: no real demand).

- How is the price behaving on approach to an important resistance level?
  Dips seem to be shallow and little retracement is seen (real money demand: dealers are working a mountain of buy orders and buy every dip).

The answers to these types of questions will give you an insight into the market's positioning and let you adjust your trading accordingly.

Those looking for more detailed trading techniques will find them in the Appendix of this book, where things such as how to enter/exit positions, set stops, and use price action effectively are addressed.

---

[2] A common option structure in the FX market is the "one touch" or "no touch" digital options, where a player bets that the price will (or will not) trade at a certain level before expiry (London or NY options cut). Thus, if the option buyer is betting on a certain level being hit, if they are large enough they will usually pro-actively gun for that level, while the option writer (typically a bank) will try to protect it until expiry so that they do not pay out.

FX TRADING TIPS

13
Adapting to the FX Market

Traders entering FX from other capital markets quickly realize that trading currencies is a quite different beast altogether and that their tried-and-true techniques simply do not work as well as they did with equities, for example. This is because the forex market's unique structure sets it apart from the major exchange-traded markets around the world, and requires most traders to go through a period of adjustment.

Perhaps the most obvious distinction (and difficult to handle for individual traders) is the fact that the foreign exchange market trades continuously 24 hours a day, seven days a week. Global commerce does not take time off, and neither does FX. With the help of technology, trading now takes place around-the-clock, and although your broker may not accept orders over the weekend, you can rest assured that the FX market is awake and that someone, somewhere, is dealing.

TRADING DIFFERENT MONEY CENTERS

This continuous market action makes it difficult for new participants to adjust to, and new traders will find that their trading style and technical analysis often needs some tweaking in order to function properly. Since there is essentially no market "open" or "closed", technicians struggle to use their candlestick reading techniques, which are often not readily applicable. After all, everything is relative in FX, and a trader's open in Tokyo is not the same as a trader's open in London. Instead of relying on exchange-mandated hours, traders have to therefore find alternative ways to break down the day's trading.

A clever way to do this is to treat each trading session independently using 4 hour charts, which lets us divide the trading day into three eight-hour trading sessions. By doing this, we are better able to see each region's risk appetite and the long trading day now becomes more manageable. Since three major money centers are responsible for the vast majority of FX turnover, this lets us accurately divide it into the Asian, London, and New York trading sessions, and each of these has its own unique characteristics and trading style.

Asia

The majority of the turnover in this time zone is handled by Sydney, Tokyo, Hong Kong, and Singapore. Because each center's banks are in active competition with each other, this creates a more fragmented market when compared to the others and translates into jumpy price action and unsustainable moves. The main players in the Asian session are commercial names (exporters) and regional central banks, both of which love to enter the market in order to dampen volatility.

London

London's "City" still holds its traditional role as the FX capital of the world, having a deep, well-developed market and the ideal time zone for FX trading. Along with London, a host of other European financial centers such as Geneva, Paris, and Frankfurt add further liquidity to the market, creating a deep market across the board with every major FX player in operation. The moves that take place in London are generally "real money" inspired (supported by large corporate flows or M&A activity), which can have big impacts on intra-day price action, especially around the time of the London fix. All of this liquidity means that the moves generated in this session are all-important, since the amount of money needed to move a market this deep can tell us quite a bit about market sentiment and positioning.

New York

Although New York comes in second to London in terms of volume, trading falls off precipitously after 12 pm. The market is at its deepest and most active in the morning "overlap" hours, when the big boys like to make their opinions known by trading yards at a time. Liquidity for Latin American currencies and the Canadian dollar (when Canadian banks are open) is also at its deepest here, meaning that if you are trading the Loonie, then you must trade these hours.

PASSING THE BATON

Although each of these trading sessions is in fact unique, their interplay creates some typical trading patterns that traders should be aware of. Starting with Asia, the day's trading characteristically opens with a flurry of early activity as dealers move rapidly to process their backlog of outstanding orders. To the yen or Aussie trader, the first couple of hours after Tokyo opens are all-important since they usually feature most of the fireworks in this session. The lack of market depth means that, more often than not, you will find Asian players testing the limits of any previous range (possibly recording marginal highs/lows), only to fall back and consolidate the move for the rest of the session since volatility-hating central banks and exporters love to turn this session into the day's consolidation session (especially if big moves were seen earlier in New York).

London, on the other hand, has always been the market trend-setter, and not just in fashion. Although the initial moves may not begin in London, this is where the large players operate and get a chance to swing their big sticks. Moves initiated and extended in London should be taken seriously since it is the only money center with deep enough pockets to overcome any "artificial" interference such as central bank interest. Thus you typically see mighty London picking a direction and sticking with it until New York enters the fray, making fading moves a dangerous sport during these hours.

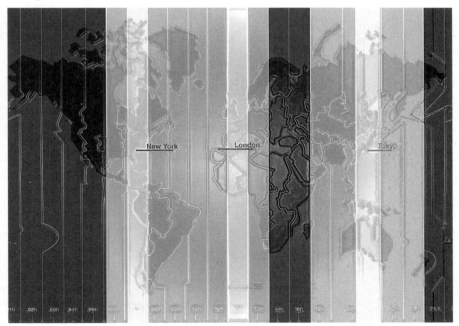

Liquidity map. Light sections indicate deep liquidity, darker ones are "thin" market hours.

By the time North America opens for business, the FX baton has been passed around and by this time most intra-day bets have already been placed. This makes New York a tricky time zone trade, since large amounts of speculative money combined with important economic releases turns New York into the prime reversal session. In the first hour of trading, New York traders high on triple espressos will typically take it upon themselves to extend any moves initiated in London, trying to squeeze out the last pips from the market before the economic news hit the screens. However, because these releases can have dramatic effects on the dollar this rapid re-evaluation combined with dealer manipulation creates some difficult situations for day traders.

You often find reversals starting in this way: at around 10 am New York time, the major news releases have been out and traded on, leaving London traders with a day's worth of profits or losses to manage. Now, if you are a trader in Europe who is about to head home for the day, you know that liquidity dries up fast after the London fix so you will begin to slowly close your books around this time. You are careful to tip-toe your way out the door instead of rushing for the exits, since you know that any rush (meaning that the original move was artificial) will flood the market with supply and turn your winners into losers in mere minutes. Of course, everyone is thinking the same thing, and the greater fool theory takes over to get the ball rolling aided by the liquidity crunch. This creates a sudden rush in activity that can easily turn winners into losers or losers turn into disasters, which is why you want to make sure that your profits have been booked by the time the fix comes around. To the nimble intra-day swing traders these late morning New York reversals are a goldmine, especially since the remainder of the day is simply spent by New York dealers handling modest flows and jockeying with the IMM guys in Chicago until Tokyo comes back on line.

Important times of the day that all traders should be aware of

(GMT)	
00:00	Sydney Open (good time for an ambush)
11:00	LIBOR Spot Fixing (manipulation)
15:00	London FIX (corporate and "must do" flows)
17:00	NY options cut (manipulation)
18:00	Europe closes their books (reversal time)
19:15- **19:30**	Close of the IMM (last minute positioning by Chicago traders)
	Manipulation and abnormal moves are common during these times, so keep your eyes peeled and watch your stops!
	Check your own local time

USING A ROLLING PIVOT POINT

One of the best ways to counter some of the technical problems discussed previously is to use a pivot point for each one of the day's trading sessions. A pivot point is that special line in the sand where most traders turn from being bearish to bullish (or vice versa), and just like in sports when you feel the momentum shift from one team to another, these "shifting points" can be used in FX to tell if sentiment has switched to being positive (long) or negative (short). This lets you get a feel for the market sentiment, and basically means that if the price is trading above the pivot, you want to play only the long side, and if below, the short side. There are several ways of calculating pivot points, with the classical one used by most Chicago boys being:

$$(\text{High} + \text{Low} + \text{Close})/3 = \text{Pivot}$$

We can use the 4 hour chart to calculate the next pivot point, so all that is required is simply to plug the values of the last 4 hour bar into the pivot formula to find the next session's pivot point, thus giving us two pivot points per session (six per trading day).

Once you have your pivot point, play the market from the long side if the price is above the pivot and from the short side if below.

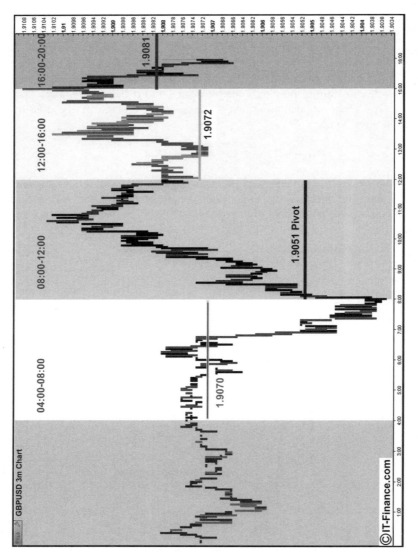

A rolling pivot point recalculated every four hours is a good indicator of market sentiment and flows.

The thinking behind pivots is simple yet powerful: if buyers are willing to pay more for the same thing today than they were yesterday (or four hours ago), then at least for the time being flows must be positive. Although you should not trade the break of this pivot, it is, however, a nice way to manage the continuous market action by breaking down each money center's risk appetite and integrating it with your other analytical tools. By applying this filter to our technical signals, we are able to only accept "buy" entry signals if the price is trading above the pivot, and only accept "sell" signals if below, etc.

TIME MANAGEMENT

Although the FX market can accurately be described as a 24 hour market, no trader can possibly hope to keep up with this nonstop action. All FX traders suffer the consequences of following the market, and you can usually identify them by the bags under their eyes and the Reuters machine next to their bed. Depriving your body of much-needed sleep is something that many new retail traders overlook to their detriment, and understanding when *not* to trade can be just as important as when to trade.

Professional FX operations keep up with the market by employing 24 hour trading desks with two or three shifts, splitting up the day's time between traders. Although they may keep some odd hours, FX dealers still wake up, go to work, and go home. Similarly, a retail trader cannot possibly hope to keep up with the whole market and must learn to manage their time accordingly (especially for those trading from home). Spending 20 hours a day in front of the screen is simply not a good way to foster long-term success, since it will eventually eat into your decision-making (and social!) skills.

New traders must become comfortable with the fact that moves will occasionally be missed, but in general all traders should try to trade the London–NY overlap, since that is where the market is at its deepest and the moves offer the best opportunities for day traders. If seen on a graph, the daily currency trading turnover would feature spikes of activity during the major money center hours and flatline near some predictable times of illiquidity and abnormal moves. San Francisco never blossomed into the bridge between NY and Tokyo, leaving a liquidity gap between 3 and 7 pm (NY time), making for thin markets and abnormal spikes caused by stop-hunting.

You want to make it a point to trade no more than two of the three trading sessions, and learn to manage your time so that you above all avoid the boring and illiquid hours between openings. Since the body is pre-wired to seek out stimulation at all times there is possibly nothing worse for a trader's mind than boredom, and instead of sitting on your hands you will find yourself needlessly entering the market in search of some action. For this reason, low-interest times should be avoided at all costs, and even if you have open positions you should simply set your stops/limits and go away. More likely than not you will find the price exactly where you left it.

14
Trading Thin Markets

Thin markets are the FX equivalent of shark-infested waters. When markets are referred to as being "thin" or "light", it means that there is simply not enough liquidity (buyers and sellers) to create a deep and balanced market. In these situations, transactions that would normally be absorbed by an active market can have unusually large and usually unpleasant ramifications on price. Thin markets are often used to run stops by dealers and specs alike, since this is when they get most bang for their buck. Thus liquidity-challenged hours (late NY, Sydney) are prone to see jumps, gaps, and generally unaccounted for moves.

How to identify thin markets

- Prices have not moved more than 10 pips in two hours.
- Prices are jumping back and forth 50 pips at a time.

Hours

- Once the Europeans go home and the New Yorkers settle in for their afternoon nap, you can actually hear the liquidity dry up if you stand close enough to your monitor.
- The late Asian session also tends to be a lot less liquid than the London or NY hours, especially outside the majors.

Events

- Before/after major news releases. It makes sense that markets would be thin right before a major economic release, since most people do not want to take a position (gamble) right before the numbers. Prices become jumpy, spreads widen, and stops get killed.

Seasonal

- Bank holidays, month of August, the week between Christmas and New Year.

How to trade thin markets

- The easiest thing to do is to avoid them.

- If holding a position, take some exposure off the table or place your stops out of the reach of stop hunters. You can also hedge your position with a highly correlated pair (i.e. EURUSD and USDCHF). The last thing you want is to have your position taken out by a single blip.

Typical price action on US data-heavy Fridays.

TAKING ADVANTAGE OF THIN MARKETS

On a Friday when important news has been released (deficit, NFP, etc.), prices tend to move one way, then the other, then the other, until finally deciding on one direction. After the big move the pair becomes O/S (or O/B) on an intra-day basis, and some sort of support has been established that will presumably hold until the weekend. This is the kind of setup that dealers love to exploit, and if you recognize it so can you.

Looking for a quick trade before the weekend, Joe Trader will buy near the bottom (see above) hoping to catch a quick over-sold bounce. He places his stops below the day's support and is in the trade more because he is bored than because of his convictions. Smart traders will recognize this level and know that before everyone heads home for the day one final stop-hunting move is probably on the cards.

After London goes home for the weekend, and about the time New Yorkers start checking their clocks, the dealers will pounce. If there are enough stops gathered nearby to garner their attention, they will quickly set up a coordinated attack and take them out in the blink of an eye. All that you have to do is identify the setup and go short with the dealers as soon as the rate approaches the support level, knowing that the support is artificial and the move should give you a quick 10–20 pip move (just enough to run Joe's stops). Since the buildup to these moves tends to be rather slow (although the actual stop run in instantaneous), it is best to simply set orders in the market and wait for the price to come to you. The first sell order would be placed at/near the support level, with a take profit some pips below (exactly the opposite of Joe's orders). Having them as limit/stop orders will ensure that they get executed since some brokers like to shift to "manual execution" when they are about to run stops.

Once the stops are filled, the price goes back to where it was, and the market proceeds to die for the rest of the day. Your profit take order is done and you are free to enjoy the rest of your Friday afternoon.

Towards the end of the day dealers easily take out Joe's attempt to pick a bottom.

15
Using the Crosses

Finding the right pair to trade should be of utmost importance to all individual traders. Opportunity cost is a real cost for most traders and funds committed to any one position are funds that cannot be used in other (possibly more profitable?) trades. Since in FX every pair is in one way or another connected to the others, traders who adopt a dollar-centric view risk missing promising trades and not understanding the real potential some opportunities offer. Although most of the dealing is done through direct dollar buying/selling, one should constantly keep an eye on the crosses in order to gauge a currency's true strength/weakness,[1] which in the end will tell you which pair is best to trade.

A very reasonable way to trade equities is to trade from big to small. For example, through your analysis you determine that the stock market in general should rise, but knowing that you have limited funds, you need to choose your stocks carefully. It would therefore be advisable to look at sector-specific indices and find the most promising of the bunch. From there, you would look within the index and find the most attractive company(s) in which to invest directly. This "big-to-small" thinking is very solid and should be applied to FX.

Even if not trading them directly, cross movements should never be overlooked, since the movements of the crosses can often hide the footsteps of large players choosing to position themselves in a stealthy manner rather than through one of the majors. If someone is looking to load up on euros, for example, they may try to fly under the radar by buying euros against Swiss francs, sterling, yen, or other more obscure crosses. These are bets on broad-based euro strength (for fundamental reasons) spread out over a number of currencies (a basket) rather than taking a direct dollar negative position.

The crosses can also prove incredibly important to swing or momentum traders, since they can be used as forecasting tools and show you which currency is leading

---

[1] I personally do not like to use the USD Index (USDX) to gage the USD's broad strength/weakness, since the basket is heavily euro-weighted and essentially makes the index a mirror of the EURUSD.

the pack. Traders that overlook the importance of the crosses are often stuck with positions that do not move, while the rest of the market takes off in their desired direction.

PRESSURE VALVES

If the dollar is rallying against everything, but cable does not seem to be moving much, then one look at its crosses will show you where the selling pressure is being absorbed. Maybe sterling is rallying strongly against the euro or against the yen; in the end it does not matter. All that matters is that your cable short is barely in the black, and probably poised to bounce back strongly when the demand for dollars is exhausted.

With limited funds you always want to pick the pair that will move the most, but how exactly do you come to a reasonable conclusion? That is where the crosses come in.

Cross movements either work to amplify the move or minimize the effects. If the euro is dropping against the dollar, for example, but rising against the pound, the net effect will be to limit the size of the EURUSD fall. When this cross is rising, it is telling us that the euro is outperforming the pound, and vice versa.

Look at an example below of using the crosses. You are certain that the next few days will be a period of dollar strength (for whatever reason), but faced with

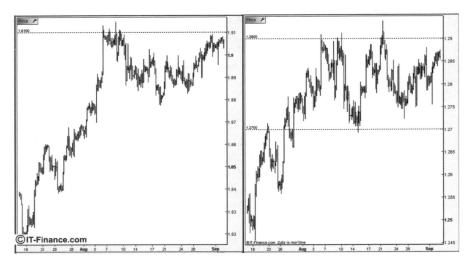

Which one to trade? We turn to the crosses for help.

It is reasonable to assume that EURGBP will bounce from the area of strong support.

limited resources you cannot take a broad-based USD bet. You only have enough ammunition to trade one pair, and decide to either short the euro or cable. The question then becomes, which one?

By looking at the EURGBP chart above, we notice that its sharp fall has it testing the area of strong support near .6720. Chart patterns and oversold technical readings means that we can reasonably assume that this area of support will hold and that the cross may stage a brief rebound. Of course we can either anticipate this move or wait for the price action to confirm our thoughts. Either way, a rising EURGBP means that sterling is likely to be the weaker of the two.

Any EURUSD selling pressure (euro sells) is likely to be offset somewhat by the rebounding cross (euro buys), while GBPUSD sales (sterling sales) will only be amplified by the cross sales (sterling sales). Since EURGBP is likely to bounce, it would therefore make sense to short cable instead of euro.

In the aftermath, we can see that EURGBP did indeed bounce as expected (see below), and the added selling pressure on sterling caused GBPUSD to drop nearly 200 pips more than EURUSD! If at the very beginning we had instead chosen to randomly pick one of the two pairs to short, we may have missed out on a great trade.

EURGBP bounces at least temporarily from its support.

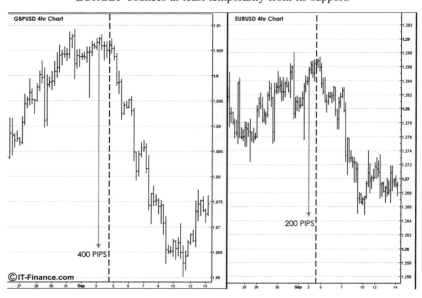

The difference in picking the right pair can prove significant!

Every trader should have currency pages set up within their charting software that focus on these key crosses:

EURO	STERLING	YEN	SWISSY
EURUSD	GBPUSD	USDJPY	USDCHF
EURCHF	GBPCHF	EURJPY	EURCHF
EURJPY	GBPJPY	GBPJPY	GBPCHF
EURGBP	EURGBP	CHFJPY	CHFJPY

Looking at the cross charts in a daily and 4 hour time frame will instantly give you an idea of the relative strength of a currency and show you who is leading the pack in the near term.

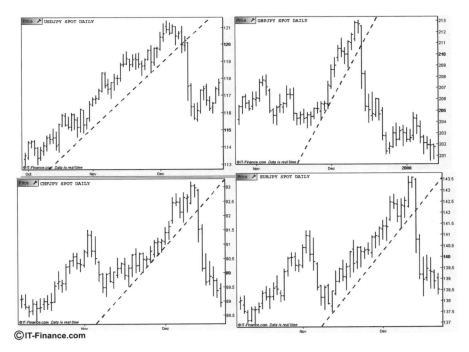

Looking at a yen page, we can instantly see that the yen strengthened across the board, confirming the yen as the primary driver. If some of the charts were dropping and some were rising, on the other hand, this would indicate that the market was concentrating on another currency.

16
All About Stops

Does active stop hunting really take place? Of course it does! Dealers are as much information peddlers as they are price quoters, and every dealing desk has their partners in crime: either important clients or other friendly desks to whom they communicate their client's positions and stops. Stop hunting takes place all day, every day, and there are some prop desks that actually specialize in hunting for stops for short-term gains. Sometimes no communication is needed, since dealers know that Joe Trader places his stops at such obvious levels that they become perfect targets.

It is amusing to see that most brokers actively preach to their clients the value of placing tight stops as a way to control risk, but in reality they are just looking for stop levels to shoot for. Tight stops more often hurt the trader than they help him, since the intra-day FX market is filled with random moves (noise) that routinely wipe out the retail crowd's 10 pip stops.

Like all players in the market, stop hunters have limited ammunition and are prone to act during certain market hours in order to achieve the maximum effect. Illiquid or extremely volatile times enable operators to easily manipulate prices in the short run, either by quoting off-market prices or by moving the market with large orders. Thin market hours are especially vulnerable to manipulation, and early Sydney and late NY should be avoided by traders. The rollover hour[1] is also particularly prone to manipulation as inexperienced spec traders place short-term trades hoping to take advantage of the rollover interest, only to see them get blown away by the dealers. Only pigs waiting to get slaughtered place intra-day carry trades.

STOP LEVELS

The intra-day FX market is so full of market noise that knowing where to place stops (or not place them) has become increasingly important. Prices tend to jump 10

---

[1]Usually 5 pm NY time, when overnight positions are "rolled over" and interest is credited/debited.

or 20 pips for no apparent reason (most likely because of flows) and retail traders often find their stops being constantly taken out even though the market may be moving in their desired direction. Ideally, you should aim not to leave any fixed stops in the market. Although professional money managers often trade with stops, they leave the orders on *their* computers instead of with their brokers (making them invisible), and more often than not trade with no stops at all. Trading in this way involves viewing your positions not as one-off trades that either go right or wrong, but rather as continuous views that are to be constantly traded around until the preferred outcome materializes (see the Appendix for tips on trading out of a losing position).

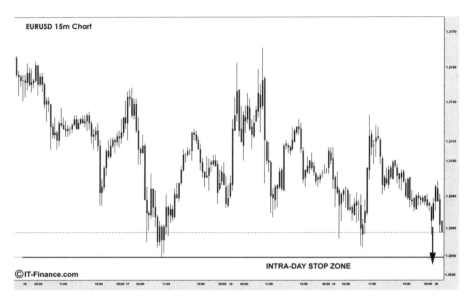

Stop hunting near an obvious support point. Dealers know the size and location of the stops sitting below the support zone and decide to go after them.

Unless trading long-term, placing a trailing stop is also not advisable since you effectively give up control of your position and simply choose to exit at a random number, which may or may not have anything to do with the price action. Place it too close and you will get hit too early; place it too far and you will forego some profits if the rate quickly retraces. A static 10–20 pip stop is also arbitrary and can actually turn a winner into a loser very quickly.

Your stop points should therefore be based on dynamic levels rather than arbitrary static numbers. Dynamic stop levels such as moving averages, Bollinger bands,

As you can see, dealers quickly trip stops, after which the price is then free to move according to regular market flows.

SARs, etc.,[2] are all good ways to manage risk while letting the market do what it does. The more experienced a trader you become, the more you will come to realize that trading with fixed stops in the market may actually hurt you more than help, both psychologically and profit-wise.

> ### Don't Feed the Stop Hunters!
> **Avoid placing stops in these situations:**
>
> - close to/at round numbers
> - before/after news releases
> - times of thin liquidity

---

[2] All indicators are readily available in most charting packages. Use default settings or tweak them according to your timeframe.

Stop hunting before news releases. In this sequence the dealers see their client base going long sterling into the news release, so they decide to take out their stops just before the number is published. If a dealer thinks that the economic data are not likely to have a big impact on prices, their tactic is to sell aggressively right before the news (using an illiquid market), trip the stops, and then take back their positions. This is why it is prudent never to enter a trade right before news releases!

17
Characteristics of FX Trends

When properly formed, FX trends tend to be particularly vicious and one-way, and routinely wipe out speculators who commit the trading sin of trend fading. It is important, therefore, to learn to identify trends early in their development and distinguish them from short-term price moves.

FX trends usually start slowly. FX trends are special because they often emerge as the unintended consequence of another action in the world's capital markets. Since foreign exchange is merely a facilitator and still not used extensively to place outright speculative bets, an indirect event such as a booming local stock market can also leave behind a massive FX trend in its wake. If Japanese stock markets are strong and global equity funds want to buy into the bull market, they will be forced to exchange their local currency for yen in order to purchase Japanese stocks. Although they are not intentionally betting on yen strength, if strong enough these flows will come to dominate the FX market. Since the initial moves of an FX trend are usually underpinned by steady real-money buying such as yield hunters, hedgers, or value investors, you have to keep one eye on the macro situation by looking for signs that the "smart money" is moving in to take advantage of a situation.

The longer the trend, the longer the correction/consolidation. Most fundamentally driven trends do not simply make U-turns. Before taking the next leg higher/lower, the market needs time to digest the initial move and draw in more buyers/sellers, or remove the fundamental reason (yield difference) in order to reverse the direction.

If the public realizes that a trend has developed, it is too late. As they say, a *Newsweek* cover is the kiss of death for any trend. By the time the general public comes to realize what a great opportunity something is, professionals have long been in the trade and are waiting to cash in by unloading on to the retail crowd.

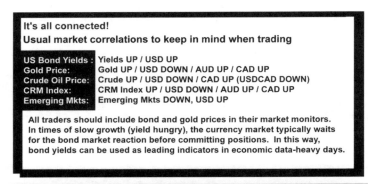

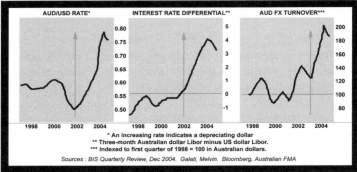

Situations like these are important for the individual investor to understand since trends are hard to stop overnight. Once the yield difference shifts in the AUD's direction in 2002, all kinds of buyers plow into the market.

In this case of the Aussie dollar uptrend, we can see a couple of interesting things happen in 2002 when the yield advantage between the USD and the AUD shifted in the Aussie's favor and set a chain of events in motion that are sometimes impossible to stop. The initial buyers of the AUDUSD are mainly yield-hungry but conservative real-money managers (i.e. pension funds), who decide to switch some of their US dollars into the higher-yielding Australian dollar. Theirs is a bet that the money they make from the yield difference will more than make up for any exchange rate losses suffered. This sudden demand for Aussie dollars momentarily pumps up the AUDUSD rate, which attracts more active managers such as hedge funds that like to play short-term trends. Of course, their buying further inflates the AUDUSD rate, which is now in a full-fledged up trend, and finally forces the hand of Australian exporters who were hedged at lower levels and must now enter the market to cover future cash flows (buying AUD). This chain of events can be clearly seen in the rapid increase in turnover and the rising AUDUSD rate, which at some point becomes self-sustaining and far from the original "yield play" that some were after. All types of players are now long AUDUSD for various reasons,

and these kinds of trends stop only when the fundamental backdrop is taken away
(yield difference) either in a real or perceived manner, and more often than not
they end in tears.

TREND EXAMPLE

Let us take a look at a real-world example of a USDJPY move seen during the
last quarter of 2005.

An extended move in USDJPY exhibits all the typical signs of FX trends.

1. Accumulation Stage (USDJPY 109-115)

From September to November, institutional and real money buyers begin to sell
yen across the board. Two things fueled this "insider" move, Japan's zero interest
rate policy and the rally in commodities. An oversimplified view of the events
would go something like this: with their zero interest rate policy, Japan is basically
giving away money and everyone and their grandmother is using the yen to finance
their carry trades. Wanting to pad their P/L before the year end (remember it is

Q4), fund managers take out yen-denominated loans and convert them into USD (driving USDJPY higher) in order to buy dollar-denominated commodities such as oil, gold, and copper for their portfolios. When the price reaches the top of the range near 114, the usual range-capping suspects (Japanese exporters) are not present, meaning that they are either fully hedged or that they expect the yen to continue depreciating.

2.   Hot Money Stage (USDJPY 115-116)

Speculators enter the fray. Momentum funds pile into the long side of the trade and continue to do so until the market tells them otherwise. Retail specs, on the other hand, take notice of the overbought readings and think that the rate is ripe for a correction since it has already gone up "too much". Those that fade the move here are faced with two outcomes: death by a thousand stops or death by averaging down. Either way, those that do not swallow their pride and recognize that they were wrong are soon forced into an all-or-nothing trade.

3.   Throwing in the towel (USDJPY 120-121)

A last gasp higher takes whatever stops were left in the market. Notice all of the shooting star candles near the top, a sign that after three months and ten big figures those holding long positions are beginning to cash out on any blips higher. Everybody seems to be long now, and the trend will seemingly go on "forever".

4.   Reversal (USDJPY 120)

In December, the market makes a sudden 180 degree turn and drops nearly 500 pips in two days. The long-awaited reversal finally came (although several hundred pips above what the retail crowd thought) as the result of some kind of catalyst that changed the underlying equation supporting USDJPY. More often than not this is a shift in government policy or some other external factor that forces the real money crowd's hand (such as a big coupon payment/redemption). In this case, the catalyst was the seemingly uneventful fact that the Bank of Japan raised the minimum margin requirements for the Tokyo metals market in order to limit speculation. Although it is nothing huge like a surprise rate hike, the slight change forced hedge funds to cash in on some of their long gold positions in order to meet the new margin requirements of the exchange.

Since the change was announced during the weekend, when Monday morning came around the market was flooded with a sudden, massive sell interest that soon snowballed into outright pandemonium in the gold market. The market headed towards free-fall and traders rushed to unwind their positions before it was too late, with the end result being that gold dropped *20%* that day! When the gold positions were unwound, the dollars received were converted back into yen in order to pay back the JPY-denominated loans that were taken out in the first place, and this massive yen buying caused the USDJPY to take a steep tumble. Although the margin requirement change may have been responsible for only the first 150–200 pips of the move, it was enough to get the ball rolling and shift the trend dynamics. This should bring home the fact that little things can have big implications, so be on the lookout for abnormal price moves in other markets that could have an eventual impact on FX prices.

Not surprisingly, I did not hear any comments about this gold story from any analysts, either before or after the fact . . . they probably blamed it on some technical pattern, economic fundamentals, or growth rates.

18
Trading the FED

Whenever the Federal Market Open Committee (FOMC) meets to set interest rates in the US, trading proves tricky, to say the least. These days the FED goes out of its way to telegraph the moves well in advance, so the market has switched from the nail-biting hike or no hike scenario to looking and analyzing every single word in the accompanying statement. This evaluation and re-evaluation of what the Fed actually "means" translates into a free-for-all immediately following the release, and dealers are hard at work chopping up players on both sides of the market while the FX heavy-hitters sit and deliberate whether the statement was "hawkish" or "dovish".

What should one do in a situation like this, when the price jumps 50 pips one minute and then dives 50 the next? Simple: wait for the dust to settle and let the price action guide your moves. Since traders like to limit their exposure before any FED release, the market will tend to trade a reasonably tight range the day(s) before any announcement, and these range extremes can be used effectively to trade with the dealers, and against the general public.

This is how Joe Trader would trade this FOMC release. When the FOMC announces its quarter-point rate hike (the market bought on the rumour and is now selling the fact) Joe goes long at the next tradable price (1, 2). Stops are placed at a "safe" distance and the EURUSD spends the next five minutes whipping back and forth, wiping clean any stops in an 80-point range.

After ten minutes, the pair moves higher again and Joe is convinced that this time the move is for real, so he sets his stops below the previous low, away from the noise (3, 4). Dealers see the spec market go long EURUSD so they are happy to fade the move higher and target the downside stops (5). Intra-day stops are successfully tripped, and dealers take back their shorts for a nice profit and call it a day (6). Frustrated, Joe Trader throws in the towel, and the market is free to move back within the range again.

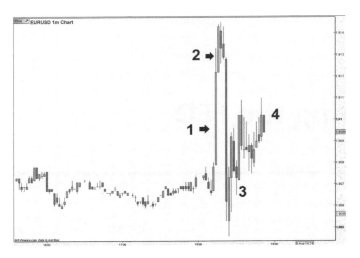

The minutes after an FOMC release.

Dealers gun for the obvious stop levels before returning to pre-FOMC levels.

This typical scenario plays out almost every time the FOMC meets to set rates, with the rate chopping around for a while after the decision until the market finally makes up its mind as to the statement. Since the statement came in with the market's expectations, the euro eventually finds itself at the same price it was prior to the announcement (even though it moved more than 200 pips round-trip!). In situations like these, when the market gets what they are expecting, then the usual scenario is for dealers to hit the intra-day stops on both sides of the intra-day range and then settle on the pre-FOMC equilibrium point. After all, if nothing changed then there is no reason for players to aggressively push the market one way or another.

THE TRADE

Trading like a dealer in this case would mean recognizing the stop-hunting push 30 min after the release and going short around 1.2820 or so, knowing that dealers are going for Joe's obvious stops sitting below the previous low of 1.2807 (see below). Take-profit orders for the shorts would be placed under the figure, for a nice 30 pip gain, which surely beats getting stopped out two or three times in 10 minutes.

Pre-FOMC, establish the range and fade the extremes.

Remember that you are a trader, not an economist. On the daily chart the wild gyrations will barely be visible, so use the 15 min charts to wait for the market to decide where it wants to go, and follow these simple dealer maxims:

Never chase.

Never trust the first price.

The trade: recognize the obvious stop level and trade with the dealers.

If the statement was in line with market expectations, fade any move outside the range and remember the typical price action: the first 15 min will see the dealers hit the high stops, hit the low stops (or vice versa) and return to the pre-announcement level before making the big move. Recognize that these illiquid markets are a stop-running feast for dealers, so be sure to identify "typical" stop-loss levels (ordinarily below/above the previous highs/lows) and go after them along with the dealers.

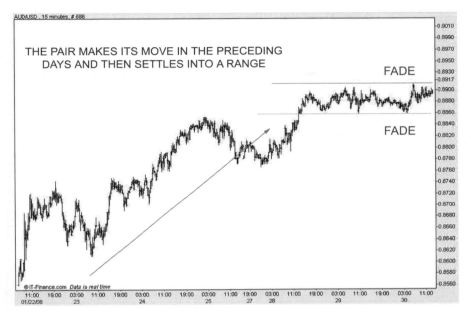

Another typical FOMC setup.

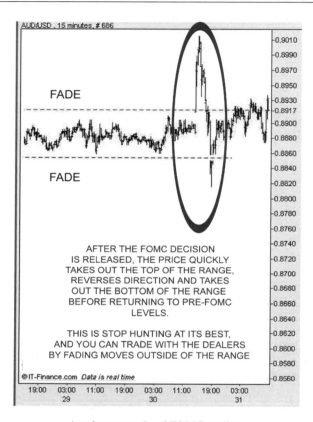

Another example of FOMC trading.

19
Fading News

In the same vein as the FED trade, dealers often like to fade "headline" news numbers if they feel that the market is still in a clear trend. Depending on what the market is focusing (growth, inflation, etc.) some news releases tend to take on greater importance than others. In times of growth concerns, an always anticipated number is the non-farms payroll data, released on the first Friday of every month.

Whenever possible, trade in the prevailing market direction.

NFP days are known for their volatility, and traders routinely get chopped up trading the headline number. It is important to note that one piece of data is generally not enough to reverse a clear trend, so even though the number may come in worse than expected, it is still preferable to fade the release and trade in the prevailing trend. Only a monumentally bad piece of data or a series of bad releases can shake a currency from a clear trend, so take a clue from the dealers and fade the moves once the knee-jerk reaction is over.

In this case the setup is typical. The EURUSD comes into the all-important payroll numbers in a clear downtrend, which will only be reversed by some fundamental shift in expectations. The following price action can usually be seen before/after all eagerly awaited economic releases and should be traded accordingly.

Before the NFP number EURUSD settles into a range as traders limit their exposure. The range limits should be seen as obvious stop levels.

Bad data (but not that bad) and the immediate knee-jerk reaction is to sell USD. Dealers are happy to fade the move higher and are soon gunning for the intra-day stops.

Since news releases and other important events are "open season" on traders, you should always be on your toes. If you find that you are at your trading best during normal trading hours, then you should think about skipping data days altogether since the initial flurry of activity is often impossible to trade, especially because retail brokers tend to shut down their systems altogether to limit their exposure.

If you are coming into an important news event with a position, it is best to lighten up and remove or place stops far enough away so that dealers will not get to them. If you are eager to trade, then wait for the initial knee-jerk reaction to be completely reversed (on 3 min charts) and then enter your desired position. Use 15 min charts to trade the market, which will smooth out the market noise and make the market's intentions more evident.

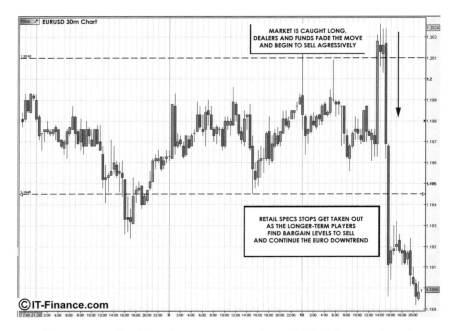

After a flurry of activity, the euro returns to its established downward trend.

Always trade in the direction of the trend. Do not assume that one piece of news is enough to reverse an established trend (or range).

20
FX Analysts: Who Cares?

As more and more retail traders enter the FX market, a critical lack of market information has led to the rise of a new FX superstar: the analyst. Retail forex brokers are hiring and promoting the skill of these guys in droves, partially to offset their client's well-founded fears of the market. Don't know how to trade? Don't worry, we have the people that can teach you. Can't tell which way the euro is going? Don't worry, we have the experts.

Analysts are master peddlers of excuses and explanations as to what *did* happen, but will never really tell you what *will*. I would love to host a trading competition between those popular retail FX analysts and some of Malkiel's dart-throwing monkeys. Rest assured that my money is on the chimps.

Sadly, it seems as if the general investing public did not learn much of a lesson from the scandals following the internet boom era IPOs. If a firm is taking a company public, do you really think their analysts will give the stock anything but a "strong buy"? A similar conflict of interest arises in the retail FX world, now littered with analysts more than willing to share their views on TV, print, or chat rooms.

Let us take a look at these guys and gals to see exactly why it is that you should avoid listening to anything they say.

First of all, who are they? Not traders, that is for sure. A look at their bios will probably show you an ivy league degree and briefcase full of theoretical knowledge. Is any of this knowledge applicable to day-to-day FX trading? Probably not, but what do they care? They have a nice cushy salary that has nothing to do with the accuracy of their predictions. Trust me, if their forecasts were so good, they would have been smart enough to start their own fund long ago.

What are their job requirements? Look good on TV and write convincingly. Basically they must be able to spew mountains of meaningless FX jargon and economic figures in order to back up their views.

So what is their job? Like any job in the world, their role is simple: to make money for the company. How do they do this? By providing traders with "valuable" information intended to make them trade more. Notice that they are always full of great trading ideas, but never once have I heard one say "stay flat". Since brokers only make money when you trade, in their opinion there will always be something worth trading. A wise trader will never trade from the advice of their broker.

I will let you in on the FX market's little dirty secret: some moves just "happen" and nobody really knows why! Since corporate flows routinely make a mess of intra-day markets, most moves have no fundamental or technical reason behind them, yet no self-respecting analyst will ever be caught without a neat explanation at hand.

Take a look at some of their great analyses. The chart below is from the Friday Non-Farms Payroll before a long holiday weekend in the US. Just by looking at the chart, we can see the price flat-lining until the payroll data comes out, followed by immediate dollar buying and then a gradual retracement of the move by the day's end. If any analyst had just mentioned that, they would have received a gold star in my book. But alas, their overwhelming need to show their FX knowledge urges them to fill the trader with tons of superfluous – and downright false – information.

Here is what one prominent FX analyst had to say about the day's events:

> The dollar immediately gained ground after the above-mean NFP numbers were taken by the macro crowd as a sign that US economic growth is not showing any signs of slowing down. Investors bought dollars aggressively across the board, betting on a strong US economy. Towards the end of the day, so-so confidence numbers forced institutional investors to re-think their strategy and they took back some of their dollar longs as the new data did not meet their expectations of a robust US economy.

Sorry? Do these people really think that insurance companies, pension funds, etc., trade off tick charts? The thinking of macro funds therefore goes something like this: "The US economy is stronger than what people thought; let's buy USD. Oh wait! Apparently it's not. I'll take back my position".

Long-term players are exactly that – long-term. One number will not change anyone's view of the economy, and certainly no one in their right mind would place a trade based on US economic prospects only to reverse them after another number comes out. Notice they did not even mention the fact that it was the Friday

Analysts will always have an explanation for the day's moves, even if none exists.

before Labor Day weekend ... meaning that it is doubtful that institutional traders were even at their desks!

If we look at the same move from a price-action perspective, however, we can get a much more reasonable (and probable) explanation for the day's events:

- From the EURUSD's rise in the days before the data release, we can be sure that the market has positioned itself for the possibility of a *terrible* number (the previous five releases had been worse than expected). The market was therefore long EURUSD going into the release.

- Payrolls actually come out better than expected, and those betting on a weak number are forced to lighten up their positions.

- As dealers begin to close their books early ahead of the long weekend, a short squeeze develops that catches the intra-day crowd wrong-footed.

- Once the top-side stops have been run, the price returns to its pre-NFP equilibrium level. No macro fund was anywhere to be seen.

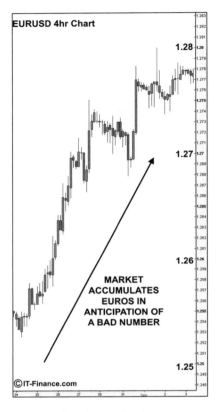

Steady euro buying.

If you still choose to blindly follow the forecasts of experts, then you may be inter-ested in a recent survey conducted by the *Economist*. The UK magazine asked four ex-finance ministers, four captains of industry, four Oxford economics students, and four garbage collectors to predict GDP, inflation, and oil prices for the coming year. Not surprisingly, the garbage collectors came in first place ... the finance ministers came in last.

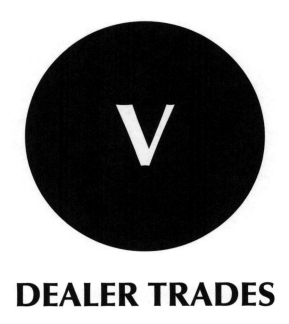

DEALER TRADES

21
Trading Against Dealers

If you are trading through a dealer, then you are essentially trading against him. It is a bit simplistic, but if you buy, he sells, and one of you is going to end up wrong. In the world of spot trading dealers have a big advantage over the average trader: order-flow information.

Imagine a poker game where you can see everyone's cards but are allowed to keep yours tight to your chest. How your playing would change! Knowing the other player's intentions would enable you to fold, bluff, and, more importantly, call their bluffs with ease. In this scenario you would be hard-pressed not to leave the table with a nice chunk of change, which is exactly the position FX dealers occupy. With the spreads they collect and the order-flow information they possess, dealing desks are such guaranteed money-makers that banks have the luxury of staffing them with tens of pimply-faced dealers who may or may not end up being good traders.

THE INFORMATION FLOW

Flow information is *the* most valuable commodity for intra-day FX traders, since in the end large flows are what shape intra-day prices. If your contacts are telling you that all they see are buy orders, then you can be fairly sure that the pair is going up. If, on the other hand, they tell you that everyone who wanted to buy already has, then you might think that the market is saddled with longs and ripe for a reversal. As we can see in the charts below, a large flow placed strategically can have a meaningful effect on prices, and a market participant aware of these flows can simply position themselves ahead of time to enjoy a free ride at another's expense. The easiest and lowest-risk trades all involve taking advantage of your customers, since by doing this you are essentially taking the risk off your books and passing it on to your client. A market maker with a big order on his book knows that it is his most precious asset and may trade the information to hedge funds or other investors in exchange for business (commissions).

The vast majority of intra-day moves are the result of speculation, rumors, psychology, and a few facts (the Greenspan death rumor is a market classic), and the larger you are the higher up you are on this information chain. If some juicy bit of information is available ("company X needs to get rid of 3 billion euros by the end of the day"), the best customers will receive the "first call", after which the information eventually trickles down all the way until you see it on your news wire. By the time retail traders get in the loop, the info has already been out and traded on, which only helps to propagate the "buy the rumor, sell the fact" scenario.

Market-moving flows are free money for the dealers executing the orders.

Getting the first call on market-moving information can be incredibly valuable to short-term traders, since rumors that some UK clearer "must do" a large cable buy order before the London fix can have a direct impact on the price. Front-running is standard practice in the FX world, and dealers with large orders on their books are keen to "piggy-back" their customer's orders to receive a quick profit. Unfortunately, retail traders have virtually no access to this information and are therefore placed at a great disadvantage. Individual traders can, however, gain access to the CFTC's commitment of a trader's report, which highlights the future market's positioning on a weekly basis (www.cftc.gov). Although it may seem a bit dated, the weekly report will highlight any extreme positioning and can be seen as a warning sign. As a retail trader you may not have direct access to this privileged

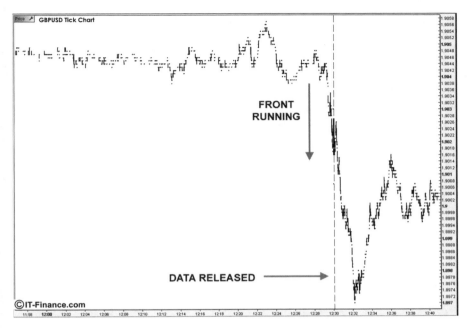

Front-running news releases. Traders with privileged information sell seconds before the news is released and get a quick 20 pip head-start on the competition. Just another facet of the FX market.

information, yet the price action before the fixing times can also provide clues into a dealer's intentions.

Most FX operations trade on at least some flow information, and for many professional traders a typical day might start like this. Get into the office, quickly glance at what Tokyo did, have a chat with the overnight desk, then get on the phone and start making the rounds. Who's doing what? Where do you see stops? Etc. The responses may be anything from "dead market" to "these Russian guys have been buying all day" or "a yard of stops sitting under the figure". A couple of calls like that and you have a fair idea of where the market stands and where it wants to go.

TRADING LIKE A DEALER

As we have seen, traders and dealers are two very different breeds and a successful dealer would not immediately translate into a successful trader. In fact, most dealers would make terrible position traders. Making markets for corporate clients requires an entirely different skill set than what is required of a good money manager, for example, yet there are things that the average trader can take from dealers and apply to their trading, especially when it comes to mentality. A dealer's "go with the flow" trading mentality and the "always be fading" attitude toward news events can be immediately put to use by the individual trader, which I have tried to highlight throughout this book.

The following are examples of dealer trades that will prove useful to intra-day speculators interested in picking up some easy, low-risk pips. According to our research, the Big Figure Trade alone has a historical success rate of over 70 %, and although rare, identifying these typical dealer setups will enable you to focus on high-probability trades. These trading techniques are intended for experienced traders already involved in the FX market.

22
The Big Figure Trade

As noted earlier, retail FX operators are at a disadvantage because they act as a trader's sole counterparty and in this function they are sometimes forced to make artificial markets. Although making markets for clients is most often not an issue for FX brokers since they simply offset their risk in the interbank market, in illiquid times this represents a big problem for them – and an opportunity for the trader.

The Big Figure Trade is one example of how you can take advantage of your retail FCM's limitations. As all traders know, every now and then the market will test a critical level. The actual level is not important, since it may be a well-defined Fibonacci level, a trendline, or more likely than not a big figure. During sharp, one-sided intra-day price moves, the market will often reach a critical level where traders believe it "cannot go higher". Since price moves in FX tend to be self-fulfilling, traders initiate short positions near that level (assuming the pair has been trending higher) and the market will immediately proceed to take them out. Usually there is a nice, big, round number that short sellers set their stops above, confident that an O/B market will not have the energy to push past the presumed option structures and the psychologically important (but often technically useless) number. In these situations, dealers wet their lips as they mount their attack on the stops.

The typical price action is for the price to fail near the figure a couple of times (heartening the short seller's resolve and prompting new shorts) before dealers produce a quick, coordinated attack on the number, overwhelming any option protection and quickly setting off the stops lying above. In an instant, the rate is back below the big figure. Most traders have had this happen to them before – a quick blip and your position is busted, only for it to promptly crash in your expected direction almost immediately. Nothing is more aggravating to a trader than this setup, knowing that your money was so quickly taken away.

This trade works especially well with retail brokers because their fixed spreads and "guarantees" force them to make a market where there is none. When the dealers push the rate higher and trip stops above the big figure, the action is so quick and one-sided (shorts forced to buy back their positions) that in the real interbank market virtually no trading is possible at those prices. Spreads widen and typically only the offer side of the quote runs higher since no dealer in their right mind wants to be long above the figure. Although a true bank dealer may not be able to get a fill at those prices, you can. Because of their fixed spreads, as long as the rate traded is there most retail brokers will fill you at those prices, just as they would have if they were filling your stops instead! This is how traders can fight back and actually use the dealers' tactics against them. The beauty of this trade is two-fold:

1.   Your risk is limited and predetermined. If the trade goes wrong, you know exactly how much you are going to lose, which is a big plus when trying to determine position size, etc. Remember that money management should always be at the forefront of your trading decisions.

2.   You get to be a thorn in the side of the dealers, which you should consider as bonus points.

Pulling off this trade requires identifying the setup, knowing the dealer's game plan, and staying one step ahead of them.

The setup.

Step 1. Identify the Setup

Look for one-way trending markets, O/B readings, obvious targets (round number). Know your dealer's game plan. You know what they want to do, so trip stops above 150.00 and collect some quick pips. As soon as the stops are tripped, the price will quickly drop back below the figure.

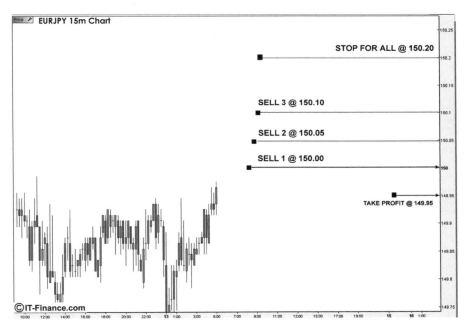

Set your orders beforehand to profit from the quick move.

Step 2. Set Your Orders

Sell 1 at the figure, sell 2 at 5 pips over the figure, sell 3 at 10 pips over the figure. Stops for all are set at 20 over the figure, with a profit take for two-thirds at 5 pips below the figure. If all goes well, you should be short a total of 6 at 150.06 (position size will vary according to your account). Risk for this trade is 14 pips. Profit take is 11 pips.

Wait a minute! What happened to the money management that I have been preaching all along? Is it completely out of whack on this trade? Not exactly.

Because of high probability of this trade working out in your favor, it is better to take the quick profit than risk losing it all by waiting for a deeper correction. We know the price action (spike higher to trip stops, then a quick decline), and that is what we are trying to exploit. Remember that we are trying to take advantage of the dealer's actions, not predict the future. The last third is left on the table in case you did happen to pick the top, although more often than not the rate will continue in the prevailing direction.

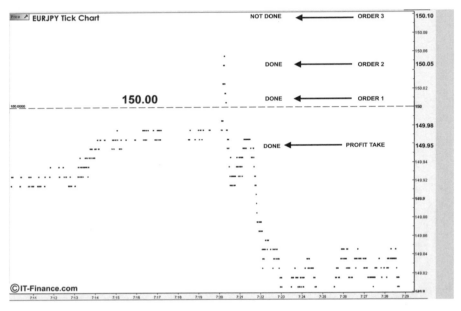

The aftermath: price action is typical. Dealers make a quick move beyond 150, stops go off, and the price trades briefly over 150 (only a couple of ticks) to print a high of 150.06. We only get filled on 2 out of our 3, and the price quickly drops under the big figure. Our profit take at 149.95 is then executed for a quick profit. Not bad for ten seconds of work!

KEYS TO THE TRADE

- Be prepared ahead of time and stay vigilant. If the trade does not work out immediately (maximum 15 min) then get out. The price action is telling you that the move is supported by real-money demand, not just dealer initiated.

- Although the moves are similar near most round numbers, this trade works best at the end of an O/B intra-day trending move, coupled with psychological numbers like 1.20, 150.00, 2.00, etc.

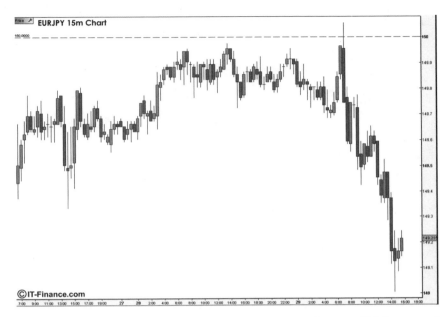

This time we get lucky and the rate slumps well below our profit target. Holding on to that last third lets you take advantage of these situations.

The trend is still definitely up (below), so do not even think about fading the move higher. All that we were looking for was a quick, easy trade.

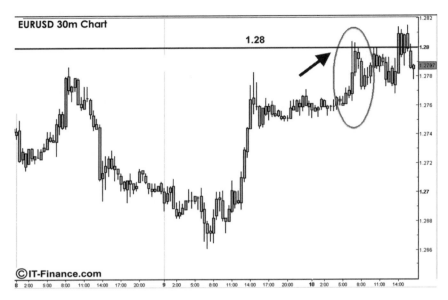

A Big Figure Trade example on EURUSD. Notice the run-up to 1.28.

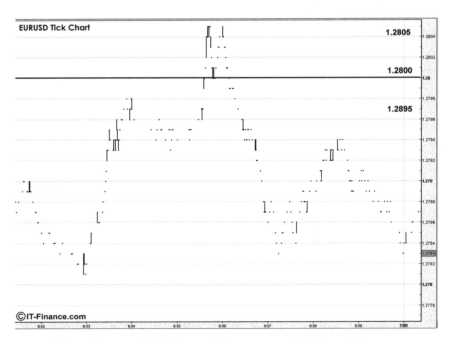

Price action near the big figure is the same; a quick blip and it is over.

Big Figure Trade example on USDJPY.

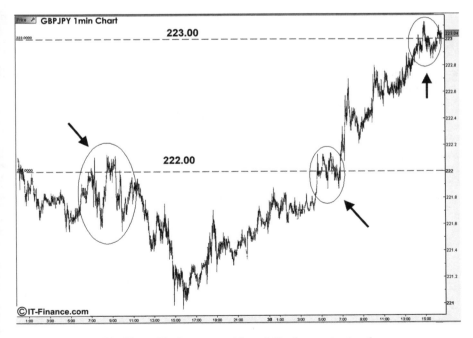

Big Figure Trade opportunities within the greater trend.

Close but no cigar!

- Remember that we are not here to predict the future (reversal or continuation?); we are simply riding the dealer's coat-tails. It might continue higher for another 50 pips; it might top-out and collapse. Either way we do not care; we are in it for the low-risk 10–15 pips that the dealers are generous enough to cough up for us.

- Generally, we only want to trade the first stab above the big figure, since that is the one hiding the stops.

23
The Friday to Sunday Extension

Another typical FX pattern that can be exploited by traders is the Friday to Sunday price extension. This simple yet by-and-large correct assumption is the fact that prices will open the new trading week (Sunday NY time) in the same prevailing direction as they closed on Friday evening. After the weekend, Sydney traders generally do not have the oomph or desire to reverse any meaningful decline seen in NY, and are therefore happy to see prices steadily drift in the direction NY left them until Tokyo comes on-line. Most of the time this behavior is not something to trade actively, but rather something to keep in mind if nursing positions or entering a late Friday trade, meaning that traders should not rely on a miracle reversal on Sunday to get them out of a jam. Once Tokyo and London enter the market the direction may be reversed, but often those traders nursing losing positions will have already been stopped out.

After a Friday with extreme volatility, however, this typical pattern is enhanced and turns into a low-risk trade opportunity for traders. The reason this trade works is simple. On economic data-heavy Fridays, prices often end up several hundred pips away from where they started the day and leave Sydney dealers with a mess on their hands by the time they get to work early Monday morning. As they go through the motions of processing the outstanding orders that the moves in NY have created, this activity often shows up as a Sunday morning "bump" created by dealers trying to fill their orders in a thin market.

This scenario is illustrated above. A big economic number released in the NY morning causes prices to jump wildly in both directions (1). Eventually, the market settles on a direction and proceeds to follow it for the rest of the day, and once European traders go home liquidity quickly dries up and NY traders begin to plan their weekends. In this 3–5 pm window, the price will thus slowly trickle in the same direction until the close of the week (2). Although you may have some late-minute stop hunting by dealers, it will be in the same general direction since

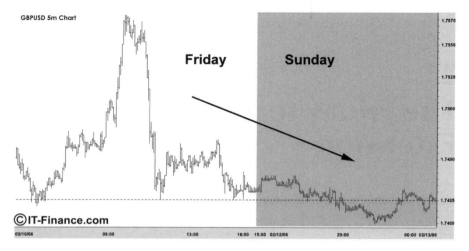

Typical price action seen after a volatile Friday; price continues to move in the same direction until Tokyo comes on-line.

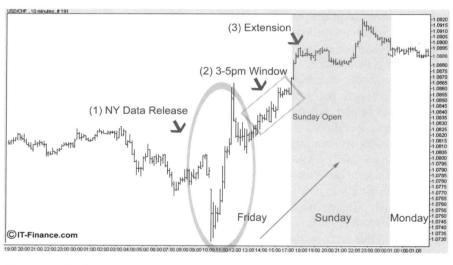

The pattern is always the same: volatility spike, pre-weekend window, Sunday extension.

the market is too thin to stage any kind of meaningful reversal. This window of opportunity enables traders to safely enter the market in anticipation of a Sunday extension, confident that they will not be stopped out before then. When Sydney opens the new trading week, the move is quickly extended a further 20–30 pips before settling in for the Tokyo open (3).

By entering in the general market direction during the 3–5 pm window, you can position yourself ahead of the market and probably against most retail traders. If cable had a dramatic Friday selloff in NY and dropped 300 pips for the day, conventional wisdom would state that the market was deeply oversold and due for a rebound. If forced to choose, most traders would prefer to take the long side, when in reality the probability is much higher that the pair would continue to trade in the same direction (at least until the Tokyo open). This high-probability outcome combined with a limited downside gives this trade great risk–return characteristics.

Trading the Friday to Sunday extension is simple, yet highly effective. All that you have to do is close your eyes, enter in the prevailing market direction during the 3–5 pm window, and return on Sunday evening (NY time) to collect your 10–30 pips. Talk about making your money work while you sleep!

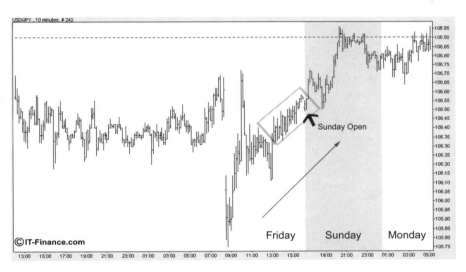

The extension is visible in most USD pairs, and can be actively traded by entering the market during the 3–5 pm window. When the market opens again in Sydney, make sure to get out with your pips before Tokyo joins the fray.

KEYS TO THE TRADE

- Don't be foolish enough to catch a falling knife; trade with the dealers, not against them.

- Since the economic news released impacts the USD, make sure to trade USD pairs only. Other crosses may trade in a wider and choppier range, which increases the downside risk.

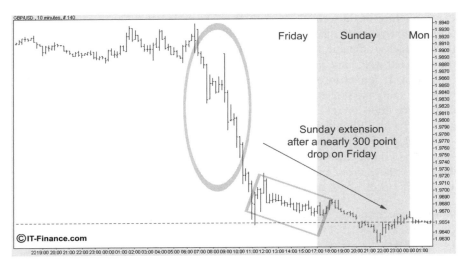

After a big day in NY, Sydney dealers are left with a mountain of outstanding orders that they have to process in a thin market.

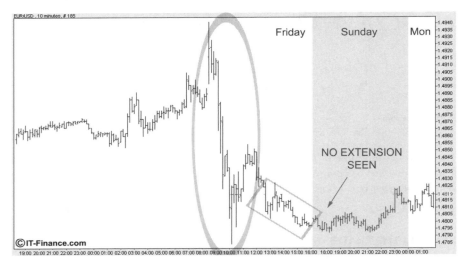

Thankfully, the dynamics of this trade limits its downside. Even when no price extension is seen, the lazy Sunday market will enable you to exit at cost or with a small loss.

- Don't trade the AUD or NZD crosses since you want to focus on thinly traded pairs and they are at the height of liquidity during these times.
- To limit your downside, make sure that no important news events are scheduled to take place during the weekend (G7 meeting, elections, etc.) since these could have huge ramifications on price.

24
Sticking it to Your Dealer

Traders shudder at the mention of the term "slippage", since it implies getting a terrible fill. The amount of slippage a trader receives often depends on the counterparty, who may either have slow dealers or difficulty finding liquidity in volatile markets, both of which can exacerbate the problem. Either way, slippage is a matter-of-fact problem in most fast-moving or illiquid markets, and as you may have noticed it usually goes against the trader.

When was the last time you heard: "Your buy order was actually filled five points lower, sir"? I'm guessing never. This is because in the case of any gaps or large sudden price swings, the dealers pass along the cost to the client but pocket the difference if it gaps in your favor (you had a buy order at 30 but it gapped down from 40 to 20, never trading in between). The advent of on-line FX brokers and their "guaranteed" orders were supposed to change that, since the extra profit margin by way of inflated spreads would more than make up for any short-term losses suffered by the brokers. A couple of years back, during one particularly nasty NFP release, a prominent retail broker stuck to their guaranteed execution policy even as prices jumped 300 pips, and quick-fingered speculators took them for a cool $5 million in the process. Needless to say, after that day the guarantees soon went the way of the Dodo.

There may not be any more guarantees, but the reasons for the broker's losses still exist, and you can take advantage of that weakness. As we saw in the Big Figure Trade, on-line FX brokers need to make a market for their customers, even in illiquid times. Ordinarily, the price they quote you is a synthetic rate created by taking the bid/ask of the quotes they receive from their counterparties, and although their pricing engines are all fully computerized and calculate at blazing speed, their quotes are still not *quite* as fast as the quotes they receive. Thus, there is a small price lag between their prices and the actual interbank market, which is referred to as price latency. To the smart trader, this is the equivalent of a time machine.

Imagine if your brokerage firm let you trade off the 15 min delayed quotes from your TV while you were looking at live prices. That would be a money-making proposition to say the least.

After performing a brief review of several retail forex platforms (there are now dozens), one can immediately notice a discrepancy in pricing. When compared to a live EBS feed, some prices are relatively fast, others are slow. This lag can become a big inconvenience if you are trying to get out of a profitable position (since their price will be slow to catch up or, worse, never even trade there), but it can become a big advantage when entering a position.

In normal trading the price lag is nothing to get excited about, since the price may be a pip or two away from the actual interbank price. In times of high volatility, however, the discrepancies can become large and inviting for the cunning arbitrageur. In volatile markets the retail pricing engines have a tough time creating a price since liquidity is thin and their inputs (the prices they get) may be all over the place, making it impossible for them to create a proper price. In times like these, true interbank dealers simply widen their spreads to limit their exposure, but retail brokers stuck with fixed spreads resort to either freezing their prices or switching to manual (dealer-controlled) execution.

After a couple of seconds or minutes the flows smooth out and pricing returns to normal, but by that time you may have already walked away with a handful of risk-free pips. In theory everyone should be able to do this very easily and consistently, although it does take a degree of patience and diligence that may not be everyone's cup of tea.

Here is how it works:

Step 1. Identify a Faster Price Feed Than Your Own

This can easily be done by placing different platforms (demo or real) side by side and comparing their performance during news events and generally volatile times. You can also choose to receive a direct Reuters or EBS feed (through Bloomberg), but that is usually not cost-effective for the small trader.

Step 2. Place the Fast Feed Alongside Your Slower Tradable Feed

If you find that your own platform is the fastest, then you might want to consider switching to one of the slower ones to take advantage of this situation. I have found that UK-based forex brokers tend to quote faster prices than their US rivals, since they often use a modified Reuters feed for their pricing engines.

Step 3. Pick the Hell out of Them

I tested this strategy by opening an account with one of the NY-based forex retail platforms and traded alongside a Reuters feed. In one week of trading I managed to collect more than 200 risk-free pips. No princely sum, but there is no reason not to take it if the market is giving it away.

Obviously the brokers are aware of this situation, and they are constantly trying to upgrade and speed up their price engines. Often they are forced to take pro-active measures when faced with volatile trading, and the first thing they do is anticipate volatile, and possibly hazardous, times. This means that at 08.30 NY time they switch to manual prices, and if 'important' numbers are due they may protect themselves by simply rejecting all incoming trades. Trading becomes impossible in times like these. This is another dirty trick played on FX traders by retail brokers. Is this legal? Of course it is!

FEED 1	FEED 2 10:00:00	FEED 3
EUR/USD 1.27 **74/78**	EUR/USD 1.27 **72/76**	EUR/USD 1.27 **71/74**
GBP/USD 1.89 **89/91**	GBP/USD 1.89 **91/96** BID/ASK	GBP/USD 1.89 **85/90**

FEED 1	FEED 2 10:00:04	FEED 3
EUR/USD 1.27 **81/82**	EUR/USD 1.27 **82/85**	EUR/USD 1.27 **72/75**
GBP/USD 1.89 **96/98**	GBP/USD 1.89 **97/02** BID/ASK	GBP/USD 1.89 **85/90**

Side-by-side comparison of three tradable price feeds before economic news hit the wire. You can see the arbitrage opportunities created by a slow feed, which lets you buy euros nearly 10 pips below market price immediately following the news release.

If your broker is quoting you delayed prices it is *their* problem, not yours. Do not think twice about taking some risk-free money from the brokers, since with their inflated spreads, stop hunting, and generally unfair attitude they are robbing the average trader blind. Consider this to be payback time for all of those stops that were needlessly run and the horrible fills you received. Although you may get pegged as a "picker" after a while, why not make a few bucks in the short run?

What a difference a pip makes!

Spreads are often overlooked by individual traders as simply "the price you pay to play", but even a one pip difference in a spread can have a big impact on an active trader's returns.

Calculating the cost of trading:

Active trader trades 5 times a day
250 trading days/year
Each position is opened and closed (x2)
Account size is $50000
Position size is $200000 (leverage 4)

This trader's annual turnover is thus: 5 * 250 * 2 * 200000 = $500 million

Now let's calculate what your broker pockets
(annual turnover * spread)/2 = spread cost

3 pip spread	2 pip spread
(500M * 0.0003)/2 = $75000	(500M * 0.0002)/2 = $50000

The cost of trading with a 3 pip spread vs. a 2 pip spread is $25000, or 50% of the account equity! Transaction costs are the number one reason why active traders typically fail in the long run (in any market). An active trader would have to generate $75000 in profits (150% return) simply to break even. Meanwhile, traders are convinced by their FCM that FX trading features no "commissions" and the cost of trading is minimal.

Source: OANDA. *FX Trader's Bill of Rights.* 2000

KEYS TO THE TRADE

- Be on the lookout for news events that are not "obvious" and time-defined, such as Fed speakers, consumer confidence numbers (generally come out in a 15 min time window), and second-tier economic news like the Beige Book, etc. One can also take advantage of their slower prices during normal market moves, which are sometimes quick and brutal.

- Try targeting more exotic pairs, which are not monitored as closely by the dealers. Most big houses have a euro desk and a Sterling desk, but few houses have a Kiwi desk, for example. Price discrepancies in exotics are less easily noticed by dealers, and may last for a while until they are corrected. (I once caught my broker sleeping and was able to buy GBPJPY 30 pips below the actual market price!)

- To enter the trade, look for the discrepancy to be large enough to at least cover the spread, giving you a risk-free trade. Normally, all trades should be closed out rather quickly, but on the rare event that you jump on to a big move take some profit and place a stop at entry for the rest and see how far it goes!

- Remember to take a screenshot of your open trade just in case your broker decides to "take back" the trade.

THE FUTURE

25
The End of the Beginning

From a big-picture perspective, the two great problems facing the FX market are liquidity and correlation. Although your trading platform's marketing may paint a rosy picture of increasing volumes, limitless liquidity, and countless counterparties, the reality is a little harsher. Liquidity is not increasing in the markets; it is either staying the same or more likely is declining. There is simply a finite amount of liquidity to go around, and although the methods of accessing this pool have increased, the actual amounts available to trade have essentially stayed the same. All of the new electronic prime brokerages and dealing services are now tapping the same well that has long been controlled by a few of the largest banks. With more and more platforms now granting access to this fixed amount, it may create the illusion of increased liquidity (you now have three price providers instead of one), but in fact they are simply slicing up the pie into smaller and smaller pieces.

This never seems to be an issue in good times and overall positive sentiment, but in times of turmoil it can prove deadly as moves tend to get magnified. News events that once failed to inspire traders are now turning into market-moving events that dry up liquidity and produce sharp intra-day swings, creating ever-more choppy trading conditions. Although the volatility may prove momentary, a sleepy market is often the most dangerous one for traders, and at the time of this writing the forex market has been sleeping for a bit too long.

The new millennium has so far been characterized by a framework of low volatility in which some currencies remain essentially pegged to the US dollar (most notably the Chinese renminbi), which some are calling Bretton Woods II. In an effort to dampen exchange rate volatility and spur global growth, central banks have so far mostly coordinated their policy moves and moved together hand-in-hand. For them, this low volatility has had the added benefit of driving many speculators out of the FX market, since in theory if all countries successfully target 3 % inflation they will all end up with the same interest rates (effectively killing currency speculation). This level of cooperation and low volatility is not very likely to last in the long run, however, and the dramatic trade imbalances we see today should sooner or later translate into a rocky period. BWII will be severely tested when these imbalances are eventually corrected and the liquidity issue will once again jump to the forefront of trader's minds.

In our increasingly interconnected financial world, when markets drop traders now say that "the only thing to go up is correlation", and in a time when traders across the globe can instantly sell whole portfolios (i.e. emerging markets) at the hint of a problem, it is no wonder that all eyes are now on China. Their mountain of dollars has essentially become a leveraged play on the US consumer, and if the outcome of this game leads to the death of the US dollar then a series of events are likely to take place that could prove harmful to the FX industry.

Instead of actually addressing the core problems facing the country, politicians will predictably choose to take the easy way out and vilify you, the trader, and implement over-the-top regulation. Currency speculators be warned!

All of this is far from certain, of course, but if currency fluctuations do indeed become more extreme then it is not hard to imagine some sort of exchange controls being implemented in the US that would limit the average person's ability to move and exchange dollars freely. This would prove to be a sad state of affairs, but politicians tend to reach for the closest scapegoat, and FX speculators will at some point in the future fall into this role. It is for this reason that I urge all readers to open and fund an overseas bank account. It is completely legal (you must report it to the IRS) and it will offer you a way to diversify your savings and tap the world's markets even if exchange controls are implemented down the line. The honeymoon period for retail FX is coming to an end, and traders should prepare themselves in advance of any future legislation.

Currency trading should not be the realm of mega-banks and billionaires; everyday people should also actively participate in the market. I would even argue that most people simply do not have a choice. In our interconnected global world, you are going to be affected by exchange rate moves whether you like it or not, so you may as well play a pro-active role in securing your future. Whether spot trading on a margin basis is the right way to go about it is debatable, but all investors should find some way to hedge or speculate on currencies, either through a foreign bank account, ETF, or an FX trading account. In the end, the way you choose to participate is up to you and should reflect your needs and goals.

IT IS UP TO YOU

Where will the dollar be a year from now? Frankly, nobody knows. Although there is plenty of money to be made in forex trading, it is definitely not in currency forecasting. In order to reach this pot of gold you have to be able to find an approach that accurately trades market corrections rather than predicts them, since technical and fundamental analysis are simply not enough to beat the crowd.

The secret to success is actually not such a big secret. Everyone knows that with proper money management and a half-decent strategy you can make money. Yet most still find themselves failing.

To become truly successful, if you are a beginning trader you should immerse yourself completely (and I mean completely) in the subject in order to find your edge. If you are already a winning trader, then you had better make sure that you understand exactly what your edge is. What is it that sets you apart from the other 90 % of traders? Is it sheer luck or something different? Knowing what keeps you in the game is the only way to find your way back during tough times. In the end, no one can ever hope to master the FX market; but for those that manage to set the dollar signs apart and focus on the intellectual enjoyment trading provides them, a fortune usually lies along the way!

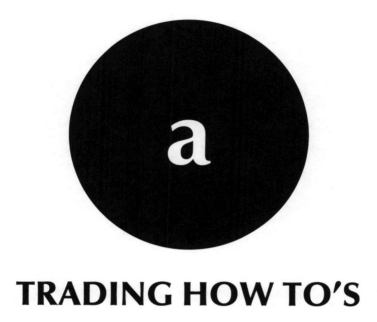

TRADING HOW TO'S

How to Set Up Your Trading

With decent money management rules and some form of trading strategy in your pocket you are ready to begin conquering the FX market. Yet regardless of whether you are trading systematically or discretionary, before you begin trading for the day you must first feel confident in your trading environment. If the FX market is a battlefield, then you are the general and your positions are your troops, and you want to make sure that you have a firm grasp of the terrain before sending any of them in to fight. Having a set game plan enables you to not only react quickly in fast-moving markets, but it also helps take some of the decision making out of the equation by pre-planning the moves ahead of time.

There are a few, simple things that every trader should do in order to stay in complete control of their trading environment.

UNDERSTAND THE BIG PICTURE

The best way to start your trading day is to begin by looking at charts from a big time frame to small. Start with the dailies, then zoom into the 4 hr, 1 hr, 15 min, etc. If you don't know where you've been, then you can't possibly know where you're going. FX trading is as much about reading the past as it is about interpreting the future, so make sure to ask yourself: are we in a ranging or trending market? Have any significant long-term patterns developed (see chart A.1)?

Only a cursory look is needed at the daily charts, but sometimes overnight moves will have created significant developments (broken trendlines, Fibonacci retracements, etc.) that will be missed if your attention is squarely focused on the short-term charts. The following steps should be taken to get a proper feel for the market:

1. Establish the general direction

Figuring out the general direction should be rather easy. Candlestick analysis and moving average ribbons (chart A.2) are elegant ways of identifying long-term patterns, reversals, or meaningful set-ups.

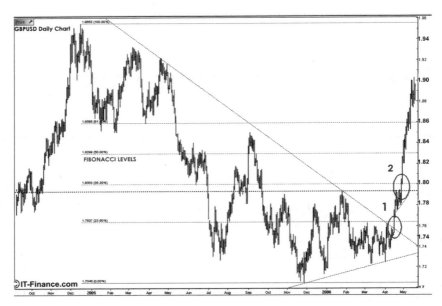

Chart A.1 The break of long-term patterns (1-trendline, 2- previous top, Fibonacci) would be missed by concentrating entirely on short-term charts.

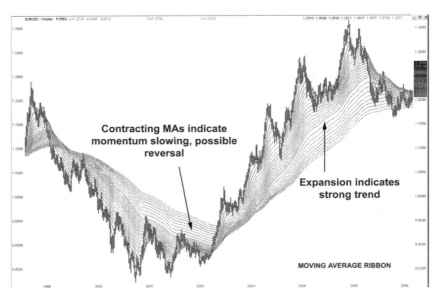

Chart A.2 A moving average ribbon can instantly tell you if the market is trending strongly (MAs spread apart), or consolidating in preparation for the next large breakout (contracting MAs).

2. Figure out the daily trading range

A good daily trading range shows you where the vast majority of the moves are expected happen, and any moves outside of the range should be viewed as short-term abnormalities that can be faded.

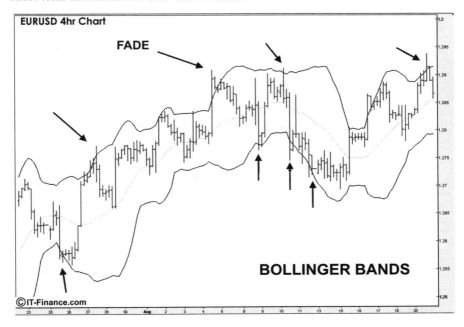

Chart A.3 Bollinger Bands applied to 4hr charts give a good indication of the day's range and any extensions beyond this (arrows) can be faded for a quick move back within the bands.

SCENARIO PLANNING

Once you have a general overview of the market, you can begin planning your trading responses to a number of different scenarios that may take place during the day. Not only does this exercise your mind, but asking yourself "what will happen if the Euro breaches 1.3560?" or "what will be the market reaction to a weak retail sales number?" also helps make your trading reaction to these events automatic.

Make sure that you know ahead of time what news is scheduled to be released, the market expectations, since all too often traders forget that there is more news out there than just the 08.30 NY releases, so keep an eye out for market moving events from Asia and Europe that may have a big impact on prices.

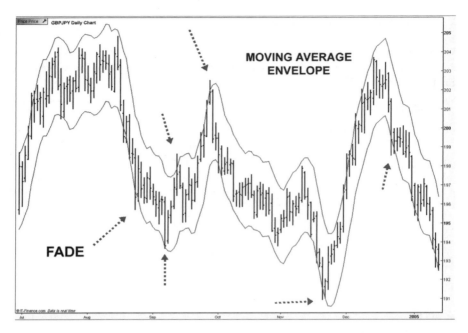

Chart A.4 A moving average envelope contains most of the daily moves for even notoriously volatile pairs such as the sterling/yen.

If after all of this preparation the price action does not correspond to your scenario and game plan (you were bearish on cable but it blasted through several of your resistance levels) then you should take this as a red flag and probably sit on your hands until you can re-evaluate the day's events.

STAY FOCUSED

Understanding the big picture does not mean understanding the *whole* picture. Since you cannot trade everything, focus on your favorite pairs and get to know them well. It takes a lifetime to understand a currency's behavior, how it reacts to things like oil prices, interest rates, etc., so concentrate on learning a few pairs very well instead of following everything half-hearted.

ALWAYS TAKE NOTES

Although it may seem like a thankless task, keeping a trading journal is the best way to reap the benefits of the analysis you have just done above. After all, if you don't keep a written record how are you going to know if your thoughts were on the money, or if your tactics proved to be wrong? Keeping a record will keep you from repeating costly mistakes ("I've been in this situation before, what did I do in that case?") since it may be hard to remember your motivations for entering a trade post-fact. At the end of the day you are your best teacher, and before going home for the day you should make sure to write down your feelings on the majors and set some targets for the overnight market. This will create a continuity of thought and help you jump back into the market the following morning. You can also use this to fine-tune your forecasting and technical abilities.

How to Trade Price Action

The sharp moves often seen in the FX markets can be difficult to trade and properly adjust to, even for advanced traders, but learning to read and interpret the price action in situations like these gives us a big leg-up. In a steep decline, for example, one must be careful to measure the reaction of the longs to know if the move has a chance to turn into a rout. By looking at the reaction of the longs as soon as the rate begins to extend south, you may be able to determine if the market is sitting on a large number of long positions or not.

Usually, if a spike lower is followed by a sharp V-shaped recovery, then you should be wary of shorting the pair. Masses of buyers entering the market at lower levels tells you that the market is not particularly long, and the lower prices represent "bargain" levels for those wishing to accumulate long positions.

On the other hand, if after the initial move lower any uptick is sold into, you can be fairly sure that the market is caught long and wrong. The longs realize that they hold bad trades, and are eagerly awaiting any uptick to offload some of their positions. This is when smart traders and dealers smell blood and go in for the kill.

Take a look at chart A.5 to see how the market reacts during sharp moves.

1. Sellers come into the market for whatever reason (news, etc.) and overwhelm any bids, driving the pair lower. When the pair slows down and consolidates the move, the reaction of the market here is critical.

2. No sharp recovery is seen, indicating that the nobody considers this correction to be a "cheap" buying level, and more likely than not some trapped longs are feeling the heat. The pair moves in a steady fashion as shorts take profit, reload, and short again. The pair will continue to move lower as long as there are more sellers than buyers, and it falls until some sort of equilibrium point is reached.

3. Normally the rate would rebound a bit from this area as shorts buy back their positions, but seeing the attractive round number nearby, stop hunters and retail "chasers" join the short selling party. The pair briefly breaches the round number, takes out any remaining stops and rebounds as dealers buy back their shorts. The longs have now either been stopped out or cut their losses.

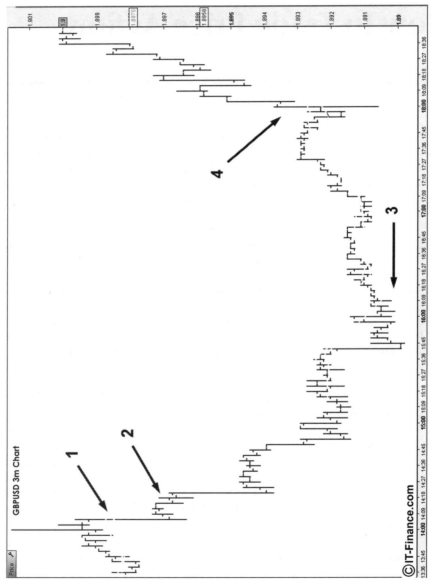

Chart A.5

After the last flurry of selling, the market is left leaning on the short side, with no fresh supply hitting the market. This imbalance in turn creates the perfect "short squeeze" set up. Since the market tends to follow the 'maximum pain' theory, it will now probably head north to try and cause some pain to the other side of the market. As soon as the dealers understand that the selling pressure has ended and the original longs have long been shaken out (remember, they have access to order flow), they slowly start to bid up the pair.

4.   Expecting a continuation of the move, new shorts (chasers) are taken on a final move lower. The market at this point is oversaturated with shorts and a sharp V-shaped recovery takes place. Like dominos toppling over, the shorts are easily squeezed by the dealers. Squeezes tend to be sharp and vicious, reflecting the panic the shorts are in. Never underestimate the results of disorderly forced buying/selling, and never fade a squeeze; lest you end up getting "squeezed".

In this case, the original orderly down-move took approximately 2 hours to unfold while the short squeeze retraced the entire move in a mere 30 minutes. Simply comparing the two halves of the chart reveals the difference between orderly market moves and forced buying/selling (stops). A testament to the power of fear.

Moves like these are typical of a purely speculative market where "hot money" is out chasing prices and no real money or long-term fundamentally inspired bets are being placed. Basically the day to day chop of the FX markets.

So how does one trade these choppy markets?

TECHNICAL HELP

Moving averages are one of the oldest tried-and-true indicators, but since they are lagging indicators to the short term trader they seem to be of little use. As with all price-driven indicators there are trade-offs, and one has to look at the MA itself to find good uses for such a tool.

The most widely looked at MAs are the 50, 100, and 200 day MA which are a simple, yet efficient ways to gauge trends, their strengths (measured as a % away for the MA), and reasonable support levels. All day-traders should know where these levels sit on the daily charts, because as widely followed indicators they attract stop hunters and should therefore be avoided.

Since moving averages essentially relate the past price action, they can also be used effectively intra-day for entering and exiting positions in one-way markets. During sharp moves, it can be difficult for a trader to properly enter a position since retracements are far and few, and the "it can't go higher/lower" mentality may set in.

For example, even though you were bearish on cable, at the end of the day you find yourself on the sidelines looking at a 200 point drop, or worse, caught trying to pick a bottom.

In this scenario, the MAs can be used as dynamic resistance levels to trade off of, with much better results than the stop-happy static support/resistance levels known to the whole market. Using the 10 and 20 you can effectively choose when to open and close your position based on price action, not just an arbitrary number. Refer to chart A.6.

Chart A.6 Using moving averages during sharp moves.

1.   The market breaks lower and you miss the initial short, but after a bearish cross you have the opportunity to enter a position once the price tests the 10d ma. This is the first dynamic resistance and should be sold into (a second can be sold at the 20). In this instance you have numerous chances to enter shorts. Notice how this beats simply selling the next break lower.

2.   Once in a trade, choose to exit 1/2; of the position when the 10 is breached (closed bar), and the other half when the 20 gives way (3). After the 20 gives way the price action is telling you that there are more buyers than sellers out there, and the dynamics of the move have changed.

The advantages of using MAs in this manner is that it gives you dynamic levels to trade off and gauge price action, rather than agreeing on arbitrary levels or your 'gut' to tell you when you should take profit. By taking these decisions off of your shoulders and turning them into a systematic ones, you are less prone to take profits too early and it has the added benefit of placing less strain on your psyche. Take a look back at chart A.5 to see how effective the MAs were in protecting profits.

How to Build a Position

Formulating good trading strategies and views on the market is all well and good, but if you don't have a proper way of entering your positions in an orderly manner then you may find your trade in the red the minute you enter the market.

SCALING

It is common knowledge that the ideal way to trade is to gradually enter a position, and then gradually exit as your targets are met. In theory this approach is beautiful; in reality most traders will find it very hard to accomplish. It is hard to add an increasing amount to your position when it looks worst, and hard not to take profits once it moves into the black. The psychological aspect is often times too great and lucky are the few that can sit still while the market gyrations make your P/L swing like a kite in the wind.

One way to get around these considerations is to take small chunks out of the market instead of going for the entire move. Taking profit in a trade is very important not only for the balance sheet, but also for your psyche. Profit taking breeds a positive mentality that all traders need, and in case the position turns around and you end up with a loss, at least you put some pips away to soften the blow.

BUILDING A POSITION

Trying to time the perfect entry/exit is a fruitless exercise engaged by traders that serves only to hinder your trading. Professional traders know that they are not likely to enter at the "exact" top or bottom, so instead they focus on figuring out the price range for their entry.

Let's take a look at a real-world example using the loonie (USDCAD):

Because of our technical analysis and interpretation of the price action, we think the loonie is poised to fall and enter a short position (chart A.7).

According to our money-management guidelines, our risk should be no more than $200 on a $10K account (2%). We have two options:

- One 100K lot with a 20 pip stop.
- Multiple mini lots with varied stops.

Chart A.7

You can immediately see the flexibility you give yourself by trading smaller lots, which is exactly the reason most retail traders should trade mini accounts. Your *total* risk should be what's important to you, not nailing the exact entry point. Most FX platforms these days calculate your average cost automatically, so figuring out the risk on multiple positions is fairly easy to accomplish.

Let's say we decide to trade 5 mini lots (leveraging 5 times). If we where to trade them all at once, then we would need to set a 40 pip stop. We are risking the same amount ($200) but at a lower risk profile. The more experienced you get with your trading, the more comfortable you will be in varying your entries and stops.

Of course, before we are even close to entering the trade we will already have charted out the day's trading levels which we can use to enter and exit the trade. With five lots to trade, we begin to enter incrementally higher amounts once our entry price is reached.

Chart A.8

1. **First sell order executed @ 1.1330**
   Just getting our feet wet, making sure we have an "interest" in the market.

Now, one of two things can happen. The more common one is to see the price shoot up as soon as we enter our short. This is when most traders scream "this always happens to me!", but in our case we are just happy to see better selling levels. On the other hand, if the pair proceeds to immediately plummet, then our position would already be in the black. Not a bad place to be. Starting small means putting yourself in a win-win situation.

2. **The loonie moves higher and we sell 2 more @ 1.1345**
   We are now short 3, and we have two more bullets remaining.

After a few minutes, the pair continues to move higher and is sitting at 1.1355, 25 pips above our original entry. If the rate continues to climb higher, we still have 2 more lots to better our cost, or if we feel uncomfortable with the trade we can choose to exit with a meager loss. Using the one-lot strategy, we would have already been stopped out.

3.   **The pair finally begins to come off and gains downside momentum.
         We enter our final two shorts @ 1.1333**
         We are now short 5 avg. cost 37.

Note that this is not "averaging down," which is a desperation move. This is
building a position. We were able to get a better cost for our short (37 compared to
the initial 30) and managed to ride the blip higher that stopped out many of your
fellow traders.

Once the topside stops are taken out, the trade now has room to move on the
downside. We exit according to our support levels, taking out 2/3 and leaving the
rest with a stop at entry looking for lower levels.

Big traders rarely trade with fixed orders in the market (for fear of revealing
their intentions), and enter and exit positions according to price action. This type
of trading is probably best suited for experienced traders with established trading
styles, while new traders are better-off trading with multiple fixed orders in the
market which lets them focus on tweaking their analysis instead.

Building a position means establishing ranges for you to trade off of, rather than
trying to define absolute values for the perfect entry. In the FX market there is so
much intra-day noise that trying to find the perfect entry and exit of any trade is
practically impossible; so why bother? Instead of thinking "at what price should I
enter," you should be thinking "what is a good 10-15 pip range to enter/exit my
positions?" As long as your analysis is correct most of the time, you should be
able to make money most of the time as well.

TRADE YOUR TIMEFRAME

Once in the trade, a crucial mistake some traders make is to trade out of their
time frame. Once in a trade, it can be tempting to scour different charts in order to
find some glimmer of hope that may turn that losing trade into a winner. A trade
opened according to the 3 minute chart will turn sour, but a stubborn trader will
not let go and turn to the 15 min or 30 min charts where the trade looks better. As
you may have guessed, this never works and only opens the door to larger losses
and more pain for the trader.

Learn to cut your losses short. If you opened your trade according to a signal
from the 3 min chart, get out as soon as the 3 min chart tells you the trade is no
good. It's no use to flip time frames until you find a chart that suits your needs;
remember that you are following the price action, not the other way around.

The only time it's appropriate to switch time frame is when the trade is deep
in-the-money. If the signal came from the 3 minute chart but extended farther than
you thought, it may be reasonable to think that the move has further to go. Switching
to a longer time frame may show you the market rolling over and confirming the

signal. In this case it is wise to take some profit and let the rest run, but a good rule to follow is to get out according to the time frame you used to enter the trade. If your original analysis was incorrect, then you can't to turn a loser into a winner; no matter what fancy indicators or software you may use. Trash in . . . .trash out, as they say.

How to Trade Out of a Losing Position

One of the most important lessons any trader needs to learn is how to effectively trade out of a losing position. Although this is usually the realm of money management techniques, at some point in their careers traders may find themselves with a trade that is deep underwater and that has the potential to wipe out their account.

Although it would be easy to note that if proper money management rules are followed this situation should never arise, in the real world traders do sometimes find themselves in these positions because of a slip in judgment, technical problem, or simply stubborn behavior. In any case, most traders do at some point find themselves with a run-away position, and what they do in such a scenario determines their longevity in the market.

When holding onto a big loser, most traders have two choices: cut the position immediately for a huge loss, or try to average down and hope for a turn around. Neither approach is particularly attractive, seeing as how you take a big monetary hit with one, or place all of your chips on the table and hope for the best with the other.

There is a third way: trading yourself out of the market. Great traders simply refuse to take an outright loss by way of a stop, and instead once they realize that the market has proven them wrong they begin to "lighten up" by slowly trading their way out of a losing position.

Once you realize your position is dead in the water, your mission then becomes to better your average cost *without* adding to the position. Adding to the position (averaging down) only creates more pain, and can quickly take away your flexibility as the loss grows and becomes unmanageable. So instead of adding, we need to cut part of it on a dip in order to gain more breathing room and be able to trade out of the rest.

Chart A.9 The key to this strategy is flexibility.

Take a look at the chart at left to better illustrate this technique. Assume that you are short against the trend and you want to get out. You are faced with these options:

- Get out of everything and take a substantial loss.
- Hold onto it and hope the pair will collapse before you run out of margin.
- Cut part of the position on any reasonable dip.

The benefit of cutting part of your position on a dip is two-fold. First, although you are forced to take an initial loss, you free up liquidity and give yourself more flexibility to react to future price moves. Any move now is a good move. If the USDJPY bounces higher, you can re-load at better selling levels to improve your average cost. On the other hand, if it immediately collapses then great, it's moving in your direction.

The other great thing about cutting part of your position is that you instantly take some of the stress away. Keep in mind that one of the most stressful aspects of trading is the psychological impact a running loss may have on your trading. Faced with big losses, most traders are keen to stop the pain immediately, and thus take needless hits.

Once you have cut part of your position, you then proceed to make small trades and slowly better your average cost. Using intra-day volatility, you make small trades to effectively trade out of your position.

THE RUN-AWAY TRADE

To better illustrate this technique, let's look at an example of the same USDJPY move that surely caused a lot of pain to many traders not following a flexible trading strategy (refer to chart A.10).

1. Around the beginning of October, we believe that USDJPY is overbought and in the process of topping out. We think the rate may fail near the 113.70 resistance level, so we take an initial short at 113.50. Our plan is to scale into the position and this is our first shot – always stay flexible.

In this swing trade, we are looking for a move back down to the 109 support level in the coming weeks. We are willing to risk 150 pips total, for a very reasonable 1:3 risk/reward ratio (risking 150, looking for around 450pips,). We realize that the market may overshoot the previous top (searching for stops), so we remain flexible and are prepared to add two more shorts higher.

2. After initially failing at the 113.70 resistance, the dollar rallies and takes out stops to print a new high of 114.20. So far it's no surprise, we knew this could happen and we take advantage of the higher levels to set our second short @ 114.10.

We are now short 2 at an average of 113.80 (113.50+114.10). Stop is 75 pips away (150 pips divided by 2 lots). Always keep an eye on your *total* exposure, since that is what is most important.

3. The dollar begins to sink as planned and the trade is now in the black. We are looking to add a third short if it breaks below the figure (113.00), since that will be an indication that momentum is picking up steam to the downside. Unfortunately the pair does not break the figure, but instead rebounds and is soon testing the highs once again.

4. During this rebound we can choose to either cut the trade at cost, or stick with it. Our gut is telling us that something is not right, but we believe the pair is still ripe for a reversal so we stick with the trade. The move might be taking longer than we thought, but techs still point to a decline and there seems to be some good supply near the previous highs. We decide to take our third (and final) short @ 114.40. We are now short 3 lots average 114.00, (113.50+114.10+114.40). Stops are set 50 pips away (150 pips divided by 3).

5. The dollar proceeds to tank, taking out stops and quickly jumping another big figure. At this point you decide to disregard your money management rules and remove your stops – *it's already up almost 600 pips, it can't go higher! The pair is so overbought that it has to correct, and I will cut my position when it does.*

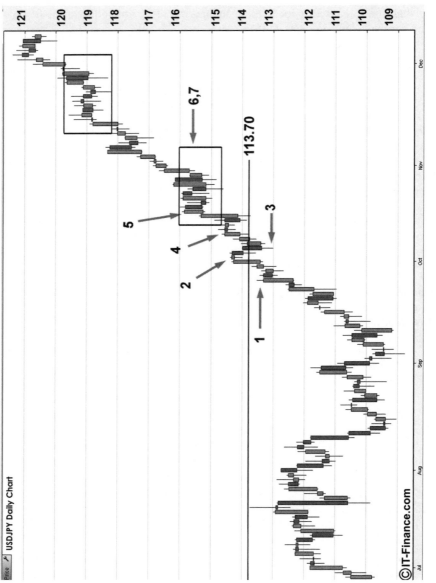

Chart A.10

Trying to out-think the market is never a bright idea, since the market doesn't *have* to do anything. Whenever the market is faced with something it *can't* do, it quickly proceeds to do that exact thing. This is because the traders hoping for a reversal are all sitting on the same trade, and vulnerable.

We know we are in trouble. We are short average 114.00, and with dollar-yen printing 115.50 we have an unrealized 450 pip (150 × 3) loss ... well above the initial 150 that we were willing to risk. This simple trade is now looking like it may very well take a large chunk out of our account, and the stress level increases. We are tempted to simply stop the pain, get rid of it all and regroup. Stubborn traders may be tempted to double up and bet on a decline.

Chart A.11

Shrewd traders do neither. After getting over the initial shock of the situation we take a deep breath, some aspirin, and decide to take control of the situation; we're going to fight tooth and nail until we come out of this trade alive.

We re-analyze the situation from an objective point of view and realize that the market has effectively proven us wrong. Pride has no place in FX trading; the market proved us wrong and we move forward. The USDJPY is not going to reverse lower to 109, and if anything, it looks like it wants to go higher.

The one thing that saves us during these bad trades is the same thing that saves dealers, namely the fact that that currencies do not move straight up (or down), but rather have a tendency to make a move, consolidate, then continue. This stair-case pattern is evident in most financial instruments, and simply indicates the accumulation/distribution stages of a move. Longs may take some profit and shorts may get stopped out, and both need time to set new positions. You should consider these consolidation periods as your window of opportunity (box 6-7).

With our new understanding of the situation we look for a dip to free up part of our position. This soon happens and the pair dips to test the 115 level.

6.   We get rid of one lot at 115.10. We take a realized loss of 160pips (first in, first out). Now we are short 2 lots avg. 114.25, with an unrealized loss of 170 pips. Taking the loss hurts, but we have now given ourselves more flexibility (and margin).

The flexibility we have given ourselves means that whatever the yen may do at this point, we can handle.

7.   We wait for a range to develop. This soon takes place as a rough 100 point range develops and trades for almost 10 straight days. We recognize that a range has developed and begin to actively trade the third lot that we freed up. Shorting near 116, we buy it back near 115. This technique proves effective and we are nimble enough with intra-day trades to quickly pocket a good amount of pips to offset some of the loss. With some quick range-trading we have put on 7 trades averaging 30 pips each which wipes out our realized loss and brings our unrealized loss to a much more manageable 120 pips. Depending on our outlook, we can then choose to either cut the whole position (in accordance to our original 150 pip stop) or continue to trade this way until a good amount of pips have been pocketed to offset the loss.

The key here is to never *add* to your total exposure, but to manage it instead. By pocketing all of those small amounts, you are effectively bringing up your average cost and making it easier for you to get out with a reasonable loss. Getting out with a small loss when originally faced with a position deep in the red often feels better than taking a profit, since you know that you fought in a market that was against you; and survived. Further satisfaction comes from the fact that you know retail traders are getting wiped out as the pair moves higher!

Remember these simple steps to trading out of a bad position

- Unload part of your position on a dip
- Wait for a consolidation to take place and a range to form
- Trade the range with multiple quick ins-and-outs
- Minimize your loss and get out. Don't try to turn a losing trade into a winner!

WHEN TO CUT AND RUN

Although you may be able to trade yourself out of most positions, there are times when you should take a loss and simply get out. If a sharp move happens for some unexpected reason (9/11, political event, etc.) then it's best to get flat as soon as possible. No one has time to evaluate the ramifications of such an event, so it is better to get out and re-evaluate later.

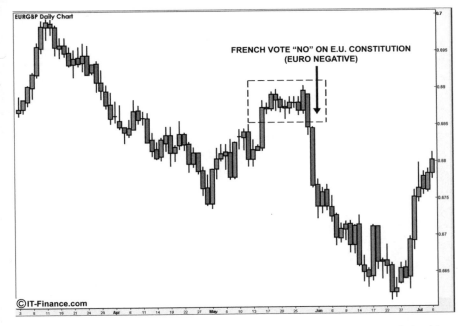

Chart A.12 Political decisions can have long-lasting effects on a currency and should not be faded.

In general, if a trade feels off at some point, then you should think about getting out. It will probably save you much heartache in the long-run. The "gut" simply represents your subconscious mind, which is constantly processing and storing information that you may not be aware of. The longer you trade, the more reliable your gut reaction will be, since it will have accumulated a vast knowledge base of charts and patterns over all those years. You've probably seen similar set-ups before but cannot remember them, and your gut feeling is your subconscious flashing warning signs. This information should not be taken lightly and good traders learn to trust their instincts.

NOTES

Speaking Like a Dealer

To new participants in the FX market, some of the terminology and parlance may at first be a bit confusing because of the nature of the market. By definition every spot transaction is made up of two transactions, making all moves relative to one another. One must be especially careful when talking about the "strength" or "weakness" of a currency, since it may be easily misconstrued by others.

For example, you are going long USDJPY but are unsure so you decide to phone up a dealer friend to ask for his opinion. He may tell you that in his opinion 'the yen is going to rise". Is he talking about USDJPY going up or the Yen increasing in value (USDJPY declining)? For this reason professionals have long given nicknames to the major currency pairs in order to clear up what they are discussing:

Euro (EURUSD); Cable (GBPUSD);[1] Loonie (USDCAD); Swissy (USDCHF) Dollar–Yen (USDJPY)

If you ask someone their opinion on the Loonie, it is the USDCAD rate you are asking about, not the Canadian dollar itself. Things get even more complicated for FX operators when discussing bid and offered prices, since they only make sense when you know who is doing the bidding and the offering (a dealer's bid and offer are the opposite of a client's). However, thankfully this does not affect the average trader.

To communicate effectively with other FX professionals, a new trader should make sure that he is well-versed in all of these terms, or risk costly misunderstandings. Also interesting is the way FX professionals interact over the phone when dealing. Traditionally, a trader may say "mine" when buying and "yours" when selling. A conversation in a fast-moving market may go something like this:

Trader: *Hi Frank, what's your price on 10 (million) Euro (EURUSD)?*
Dealer: 55/56

---

[1] The sterling/dollar nickname comes from the trans-Atlantic cable that was used for a long time to transmit prices, and the USDCAD nickname actually comes from the Canadian Loon (a bird) pictured on the side of the one-dollar Canadian coin.

Trader: *Mine!*
Dealer: Done 10 at 56
Trader: *How do you stand?*
Dealer: 56/58
Trade: *Mine!*
Dealer: Done 10 at 58
Trader: *How do you stand?*
Dealer: 60/65
Trader: *Yours! Etc.*

FX Glossary

Appreciation Describes a currency strengthening in response to market demand rather than by official action.

Ask Price Ask is the lowest price acceptable to the buyer.

Back Office Settlement and related processes.

Bank Rate The rate at which a central bank is prepared to lend money to its domestic banking system.

Base Currency The currency in which the operating results of the bank or institution are reported.

Base Rate A term used in the UK for the rate used by banks to calculate the interest rate to borrowers. Top quality borrowers will pay a small amount over base.

Basis Point One per cent of one per cent.

Bear A person who believes that prices will decline.

Bid Price Bid is the highest price that the seller is offering for the particular currency at a particular moment; the difference between the ask and the bid price is the spread. Together, the two prices constitute a quotation. The bid–ask spread is stated as a percentage cost of transacting in the foreign.

Big Figure Refers normally to the first three digits of an exchange rate that dealers treat as understood in quoting. For example, a quote of "30/40" on dollar mark could indicate a price of 1.2530/40.

BIS Bank of International Settlement.

Bretton Woods The site of the conference that in 1944 led to the establishment of the post-war foreign exchange system that remained intact until the early 1970s. The conference resulted in the formation of the IMF. The system fixed currencies in a fixed exchange rate system with 1 % fluctuations of the currency to gold or the dollar.

Broker An agent who executes orders to buy and sell currencies and related instruments either for a commission or on a spread. Brokers are agents working on commission and not principals or agents acting on their own account. In the foreign exchange market brokers tend to act as intermediaries between banks bringing buyers and sellers together for a commission paid by the initiator or by both parties. There are four or five major global brokers operating through subsidiaries, affiliates, and partners in many countries.

Bull A person who believes that prices will rise.

Bull Market A market characterized by rising prices.

Cable A term used in the foreign exchange market for the US dollar/British pound rate.

Central Bank A central bank provides financial and banking services for a country's government and commercial banks. It implements the government's monetary policy as well, by changing interest rates. The Reserve Bank of India is the central bank of India, which performs the role of maintaining orderly conditions in the forex market by intervention through various instruments like cash reserve ratio, bank rate, open market operations, and moralization.

Confirmation A memorandum to the other party describing all the relevant details of the transaction.

Contract An agreement to buy or sell a specified amount of a particular currency or option for a specified month in the future.

Correspondent Bank A foreign bank's representative who regularly performs services for the bank, which has no branch in the relevant centre, e.g. to facilitate the transfer of funds. In the US this often occurs domestically due to interstate banking restrictions.

Counterparty The customer or bank with which a foreign exchange deal is executed.

Cross Rate An exchange rate between two currencies, usually constructed from the individual exchange rates of the two currencies, as most currencies are quoted against the dollar.

Currency The type of money that a country uses. It can be traded for other currencies on the foreign exchange market, so each currency has a value relative to another.

Currency Basket Various weightings of other currencies grouped together in relation to a basket currency (e.g. ECU or SDR). Sometimes used by currencies to fix their rate, often on a trade-weighted basket.

Deal Date The date on which a transaction is agreed upon.

Deal Ticket The primary method of recording the basic information relating to a transaction.

Dealer An individual or firm acting as a principal, rather than as an agent, in the purchase and/or sale of securities. Dealers trade for their own account and risk. This is in contrast to brokers who trade only on behalf of their clients.

Deficit Shortfall in the balance of trade, balance of payments, or government budgets.

Delivery The settlement of a transaction by receipt or tender of a financial instrument or currency.

Delivery Date The date of maturity of a contract, when the final settlement of a transaction is made by exchanging the currencies. This date is more commonly known as the value date.

Details All the information required to finalize a foreign exchange transaction, i.e. name, rate, dates, and point of delivery.

Discount Less than the spot price example: forward discount.

EFT Electronic Fund Transfer.

EMS European Monetary System.

European Union The group formerly known as the European Community.

Exchange Rate Risk The potential loss that could be incurred from an adverse movement in exchange rates.

Exotic A less broadly traded currency.

Expiry Date The last day on which the holder of an option can exercise his right to buy or sell the underlying security.

Fed The United States Federal Reserve. Federal Deposit Insurance Corporation Membership is compulsory for Federal Reserve members. The corporation had deep involvement in the Savings and Loans crisis of the late 1980s.

Fixed Exchange Rate Official rate set by monetary authorities for one or more currencies. In practice, even fixed exchange rates are allowed to fluctuate between definite upper and lower bands, leading to intervention by the central bank.

Flat/Square Where a client has not traded in that currency or where an earlier deal is reversed, thereby creating a neutral (flat) position.

FOMC Federal Open Market Committee, the committee that sets money supply targets in the US, which tend to be implemented through Fed Fund interest rates, etc.

Foreign Exchange The purchase or sale of a currency against the sale or purchase of another.

Forex An abbreviation of foreign exchange.

Forward Contract Sometimes used as synonym for "forward deal" or "future". More specifically, for arrangements with the same effect as a forward deal between a bank and a customer.

Forward Points The interest rate differential between two currencies expressed in exchange rate points. The forward points are added to or subtracted from the spot rate to give the forward or outright rate (depending on whether the currency is at a forward premium or discount).

Forward Rate The rate at which a foreign exchange contract is struck today for settlement at a specified future date that is decided at the time of entering into the contract. The decision to subtract or add points is determined by the differential between the deposit rates for both currencies concerned in the transaction. The base currency with the higher interest rate is said to be at a discount to the lower interest rate quoted currency in the forward market. Therefore the forward points are subtracted from the spot rate. Similarly, the lower interest rate base currency is said to be at a premium, and the forward points are added to the spot rate to obtain the forward rate.

Front Office The activities carried out by the dealer, normal trading activities.

Fundamental Analysis Analysis based on economic and political factors.

FX Foreign exchange.

GTC ("Good Till Cancelled") An order left with a dealer to buy or sell at a fixed price. The order remains in place until it is cancelled by the client.

Indicative Quote A market-maker's price that is not firm.

Inflation Continued rise in the general price level in conjunction with a related drop in purchasing power. Sometimes referred to as an excessive movement in such price levels.

Info Quote Rate given for information purposes only.

Interbank Rates The foreign exchange rates large international banks quote to other large international banks. Normally the public and other businesses do not have access to these rates.

Interest Rate Risk The potential for losses arising from changes in interest rates.

Intervention Action by a central bank to effect the value of its currency by entering the market. In India the intervention by the Reserve Bank of India is confined to the events of extreme volatility.

Kiwi Dealer slang for the New Zealand dollar.

Leading Indicators Statistics that are considered to precede changes in economic growth rates and total business activity, e.g. factory orders.

Liability In terms of foreign exchange, the obligation to deliver to a counterparty an amount of currency either in respect of a balance sheet holding at a specified future date or in respect of an unmatured forward or spot transaction.

LIBOR (London Inter Bank Offer Rate) British Bankers' Association average of interbank offered rates for dollar deposits in the London market based on quotations at 16 major banks. Effective rate for contracts entered into two days from the date appearing.

Limit Order An order to perform a deal at a superior rate to the current market level. Can be removed on completion (filled) or cancelled at any time (pulled).

Margin The required initial deposit of collateral to enter into a position or foreign exchange trade. This is held as a deposit on any running contract.

Margin Call A demand for additional funds to cover positions.

Market Value Market value of a foreign exchange position at any time is the amount of the domestic currency that could be purchased at the then market rate in exchange for the amount of foreign currency to be delivered under the foreign exchange contract.

Maturity Date for settlement of the transaction, which is decided at the time of entering into the contract.

Offer The rate at which a dealer is willing to sell the base currency.

One Cancels Other Order The execution of one order automatically cancels a previous order; also referred to as OCO or "one cancels the other".

Open Position Any deal that has not been settled by physical payment or reversed by an equal and opposite deal for the same value date. It can be termed as a high-risk, high- return proposition.

Outright Forward Foreign exchange transaction involving either the purchase or the sale of a currency for settlement at a future date.

Over The Counter (OTC) A market conducted directly between dealers and principals via a telephone and computer network rather than a regulated exchange trading floor. These markets have not been very popular because of the risks both the parties face in case the other party fails to honor the contract. They were never part of the stock exchange since they were seen as "unofficial".

Pip Also see "point". The term used in the currency market to represent the smallest incremental move an exchange rate can make. Depending on context, normally one basis point (0.0001 in the case of EUR/USD, GBD/USD, USD/CHF and 0.01 in the case of USD/JPY).

Point (1) 100th part of a percent, normally 10 000 of any spot rate. Movement of exchange rates are usually in terms of points. (2) One percent on an interest rate, e.g. from 8 to 9 %. (3) Minimum fluctuation or smallest increment of price movement.

Position The netted total exposure in a given currency. A position can be either flat or square (no exposure), long (more currency bought than sold), or short (more currency sold than bought).

Range The difference between the highest and lowest price of a future recorded during a given trading session.

Rate The price of one currency in terms of another.

Reserve Currency A currency held by a central bank on a permanent basis as a store of international liquidity; these are normally the dollar , euro, and sterling.

Resistance A price level at which the selling is expected to take place.

Revaluation Increase in the exchange rate of a currency as a result of official action.

Rollover Where the settlement of a deal is carried forward to another value date based on the interest rate differential of the two currencies. Example: next day.

Selling Rate Rate at which a bank is willing to sell foreign currency.

Settlement Actual physical exchange of one currency for another.

Settlement Date It means the business day specified for delivery of the currencies bought and sold under a foreign exchange contract.

Short A market position where the client has sold a currency they do not already own. Usually expressed in base currency terms.

Slippage The difference between the price a trader expects to be filled at and the price they are actually filled at.

Spot (1) The most common foreign exchange transaction. (2) Spot refers to the buying and selling of the currency where the settlement date is two business days forward.

Spot Price/Rate The price at which the currency is currently trading in the spot market.

Spread The difference between the bid and ask price of a currency.

Stable Market An active market that can absorb large sales or purchases of currency without having any major impact on the interest rates.

Sterling British pound.

Stop Loss Order Order given to ensure that should your trade lose a certain percentage, the position will be covered even though this involves taking a loss. Profit orders are less common.

Support Levels A price level at which the buying is expected to take place.

Swap The simultaneous purchase and sale of the same amount of a given currency for two different dates, against the sale and purchase of another. A swap can be a swap against a forward. In essence, swapping is somewhat similar to borrowing one currency and lending another for the same period. However, any rate of return or cost of funds is expressed in the price differential between the two sides of the transaction.

SWIFT Society for Worldwide Inter-bank Financial Telecommunication is a clearing system for international trading.

Swissy Market slang for Swiss franc rate.

Technical Analysis The study of the price that reflects the supply and demand factors of a currency. Common methods are flags, trend lines, spikes, bottoms, tops, pennants, patterns, and gaps.

Technical Correction An adjustment to price not based on market sentiment but technical factors such as volume and charting.

Tick A minimum change in price, up or down.

Trade Date The date on which a trade occurs.

Transaction Date The date on which a trade occurs.

Value Date Settlement date of a spot or forward contract. Also known as maturity date.

Value Spot Normally settlement for two working days from the date the contract is entered into.

Value Today Transaction Transaction executed for same day settlement; sometimes also referred to as "cash transaction".

Volatility A measure of the amount by which an asset price is expected to fluctuate over a given period. Normally measured by the annual standard deviation of daily price changes (historic). Can also be implied from futures pricing, which is referred to as implied volatility.

Whipsaw Dealer slang for a condition of a highly volatile market where a sharp price movement is quickly followed by a sharp reversal.

Working day A day on which the banks in a currency's principal financial centre are open for business. For foreign exchange transactions, a working day only occurs if the bank in both money centers are open for business.

Yard Dealer slang for a billion dollars.

Trading Maxims

12-01-1900, NEW YORK TIMES, p. 8: If the Wall Street proverb, to the effect that "nothing is so timid as a million dollars, except two millions," is true, the timidity of fifty or seventy-five millions may be assumed to represent abject terror of any innovations involving expense and presenting unknown difficulties. *The bigger you become, the harder it is to trade*.

12-27-1913, NEW YORK TIMES, p. 8: The subject being strictly sordid and mundane, it may be permissible to quote the Wall Street maxim that "everything is in the price". *Everything is priced-in by the market*.

03-14-1931, NEW YORK TIMES, p. 43: "Good times, good fellowship – hard times, hard faces" is a proverb brought to the Wall Street mind recurrently these days... *A trader's life....*

07-18-1959, NEW YORK TIMES, pg. 19: Lorillard introduced its long-heralded menthol filter cigarette and fell 1 3/8 on the Wall Street maxim to "sell on the news". *News are anticipated and usually already priced-in by professionals, thus there is no reason to take the price higher*.

11-08-1969, NEW YORK TIMES, p. 47: The pyrotechnics in telephone and in the glamour-laden computer issues came from heavy buying by mutual funds, other institutions and market traders following that old adage, "Don't fight the tape". *Trade the price action. If the price is going up then demand must outstrip supply, irrespective of any outside news or backdrop. Always trade in the prevailing direction*.

03-05-1985, NEW YORK TIMES, p. C5: As they say in the corporate corridors, nobody ever got fired for buying IBM. *Money managers protect their jobs above all else, even at the expense of performance*.

6-17-1998, NIGHTLY BUSINESS REPORT: There's an old Wall Street saying that cash is trash. *The search for yield is constant*.

8-2-1998, FORBES MAGAZINE, p. 265: What's been going on with Amazon stock is best explained by an old Wall Street maxim: "A stock and a company are not always the same thing". *When emotions enter the markets, irrational things happen.*

8-6-1998, CHRISTIAN SCIENCE MONITOR, p. 1: There is an old Wall Street saying that the stock market has anticipated eight of the last three recessions. *Analysts are wrong more than they are right.*

8-12-1998, WALL STREET JOURNAL EUROPE, p. UK7B: Mr Manley recalls an old Wall Street saying: "If you are going to panic, panic early". *When in doubt, get out!*

9-21-1998, BUSINESS WEEK, p. 114: Grant, the newsletter editor, likes to quote a play-it-safe Wall Street maxim: "Never meet a margin call". *Never let a losing position run away from you. Cut your losses short.*

10-12-1998, RICHMOND TIMES-DISPATCH: Guy Chance, director of marketing strategy at Scott & Stringfellow Inc., recalled an old Wall Street maxim during a recent selling spree: "This is when money returns to its rightful owners". *The "smart money" always ends up on top.*

4-11-1999, SOUTH CHINA MORNING POST, p. 3: It proves an old Wall Street saying – when you rob a whorehouse, take the piano player too, because no one is entirely innocent. *Money attracts sharks.*

10-4-1999, SEATTLE POST_INTELLIGENCER, p. C3: As the Wall Street proverb says: "You can't eat relative performance". *You can't be satisfied with beating your peers, you have to learn to make money in down times.*

3-29-2000, YOMIURI SHIMBUN/DAILY YOMIURI: There is a Wall Street maxim that says a bullish market is born amid pessimism, grows up under skepticism, matures with optimism, and dies with euphoria. *Most of the people are wrong most of the time.*

Bibliography

Coninx, Raymond G.F., *Foreign Exchange Dealer's Handbook*, Third Edition, Woodhead-Faulkner Ltd, 1995.

Dewachter, H., Can Markov switching models replicate chartists profits in the foreign exchange market, *Journal of Asset Management*, March, 2005.

Galati, Melvin, Why has FX trading surged? Explaining the 2004 triannual survey, BIS, 2005.

Giddy, I.H., and Dufey, G., *The Management of Foreign Exchange Risk*, NYU Stern, 1992.

Lefevre, Edwin, *Reminiscences of a Stock Operator*, John Wiley & Sons, Ltd, Reprint, 2004.

Luca, Cornelius, *Trading in the Global Currency Markets*, Prentice-Hall, 1995.

Lukeman, Josh, *The Market Maker's Edge*, McGraw-Hill, 2000.

Marlowe, J., "Hedging Currency Risk with Options and Futures", Thesis, 1999.

Murphy, John, *Technical Analysis of the Futures Markets*, Prentice-Hall Press, 1986.

Sherden, William A., *The Fortune Seller: The Big Business of Buying and Selling Predictions*, John Wiley & Sons, Ltd, 1998.

Xin, H., *Currency Overlay: A Practical Guide*, Risk Books, 2003.

CFTC Minimum Finance Requirement

Title 17: Commodity and Securities Exchanges
Minimum Financial and Related Reporting Requirements
(selected parts)

§ 1.17 Minimum financial requirements for futures commission merchants and introducing brokers.

(a)(1)(i) Except as provided in paragraph (a)(2)(i) of this section, each person registered as a futures commission merchant must maintain adjusted net capital equal to or in excess of the greatest of:

(A) $250,000;

(B) The futures commission merchant's risk-based capital requirement computed as follows:

(1) Eight percent of the total risk margin requirement (as defined in §1.17(b)(8)) for positions carried by the futures commission merchant in customer accounts (as defined in §1.17(b)(7)), plus

(2) Four percent of the total risk margin requirement (as defined in §1.17(b)(8)) for positions carried by the futures commission merchant in noncustomer accounts (as defined in §1.17(b)(4)).

(C) The amount of adjusted net capital required by a registered futures association of which it is a member; or

(D) For securities brokers and dealers, the amount of net capital required by Rule 15c3–1(a) of the Securities and Exchange Commission (17 CFR 240.15c3–1(a)).

(ii) Each person registered as a futures commission merchant engaged in soliciting or accepting orders and customer funds related thereto for the purchase or sale of any commodity for future delivery or any commodity option on or subject to the rules of a registered derivatives transaction execution facility from any customer who does not qualify as an "institutional customer" as defined in §1.3(g) must:

(A) Be a clearing member of a derivatives clearing organization and maintain net capital in the amount of the greater of $20,000,000 or the amounts otherwise specified in paragraph (a)(1)(i) of this section; or

(B) Receive orders on behalf of the customer from a commodity trading advisor acting in accordance with §4.32 of this chapter.

(iii) Except as provided in paragraph (a)(2) of this section, each person registered as an introducing broker must maintain adjusted net capital equal to or in excess of the greatest of:

(A) $30,000;

(B) The amount of adjusted net capital required by a registered futures association of which it is a member; or

(C) For securities brokers and dealers, the amount of net capital required by Rule 15c3–1(a) of the Securities and Exchange Commission (17 CFR 240.15c3–1(a)).

(2)(i) The requirements of paragraph (a)(1) of this section shall not be applicable if the registrant is a member of a designated self-regulatory organization and conforms to minimum financial standards and related reporting requirements set by such designated self-regulatory organization in its bylaws, rules, regulations or resolutions approved by the Commission pursuant to section 4f(b) of the Act and §1.52.

(ii) The minimum requirements of paragraph (a)(1)(iii) of this section shall not be applicable to an introducing broker which elects to meet the alternative adjusted net capital requirement for introducing brokers by operation pursuant to a guarantee agreement which meets the requirements set forth in §1.10(j). Such an introducing broker shall be deemed to meet the adjusted net capital requirement under this section so long as such agreement is binding and in full force and effect, and, if the introducing broker is also a securities broker or dealer, it maintains the amount of net capital required by Rule 15c3–1(a) of the Securities and Exchange Commission (17 CFR 240.15c3–1(a)).

(3) No person applying for registration as a futures commission merchant or as an introducing broker shall be so registered unless such person affirmatively demonstrates to the satisfaction of the National Futures Association that it complies with the financial requirements of this section. Each registrant must be in compliance with this section at all times and must be able to demonstrate such compliance to the satisfaction of the Commission or the designated self-regulatory organization.

(4) A futures commission merchant who is not in compliance with this section, or is unable to demonstrate such compliance as required by paragraph (a)(3) of this section, must transfer all customer accounts and immediately cease doing business as a futures commission merchant until such time as the firm is able

to demonstrate such compliance: Provided, however, The registrant may trade for liquidation purposes only unless otherwise directed by the Commission and/or the designated self-regulatory organization: And, Provided further, That if such registrant immediately demonstrates to the satisfaction of the Commission or the designated self-regulatory organization the ability to achieve compliance, the Commission or the designated self-regulatory organization may in its discretion allow such registrant up to a maximum of 10 business days in which to achieve compliance without having to transfer accounts and cease doing business as required above. Nothing in this paragraph (a)(4) shall be construed as preventing the Commission or the designated self-regulatory organization from taking action against a registrant for non-compliance with any of the provisions of this section.

(5) An introducing broker who is not in compliance with this section, or is unable to demonstrate such compliance as required by paragraph (a)(3) of this section, must immediately cease doing business as an introducing broker until such time as the registrant is able to demonstrate such compliance: Provided, however, That if such registrant immediately demonstrates to the satisfaction of the Commission or the designated self-regulatory organization the ability to achieve compliance, the Commission or the designated self-regulatory organization may in its discretion allow such registrant up to a maximum of 10 business days in which to achieve compliance without having to cease doing business as required above. If the introducing broker is required to cease doing business in accordance with this paragraph (a)(5), the introducing broker must immediately notify each of its customers and the futures commission merchants carrying the account of each customer that it has ceased doing business. Nothing in this paragraph (a)(5) shall be construed as preventing the Commission or the designated self-regulatory organization from taking action against a registrant for non-compliance with any of the provisions of this section.

(b) For the purposes of this section:

(1) Where the applicant or registrant has an asset or liability which is defined in Securities Exchange Act Rule 15c3–1 (§240.15c3–1 of this title) the inclusion or exclusion of all or part of such asset or liability for the computation of adjusted net capital shall be in accordance with §240.15c3–1 of this title, unless specifically stated otherwise in this section.

(2) Customer means customer (as defined in §1.3(k)), option customer (as defined in §1.3(jj) of this part and in §32.1(c) of this chapter) and includes a foreign futures and foreign options customer (as defined in §30.1(c) of this chapter).

(3) Proprietary account means a commodity futures or options account carried on the books of the applicant or registrant for the applicant or registrant itself, or for general partners in the applicant or registrant.

(4) Noncustomer account means a commodity futures or option account carried on the books of the applicant or registrant which is either:

(i) An account that is not included in the definition of customer (as defined in §1.17(b)(2)) or proprietary account (as defined in §1.17(b)(3)), or

(ii) An account for a foreign-domiciled person trading futures or options on a foreign board of trade, and such account is a proprietary account as defined in §1.3(y) of this title, but is not a proprietary account as defined in §1.17(b)(3).

(5) Clearing organization means clearing organization (as defined in §1.3(d)) and includes a clearing organization of any board of trade.

(6) Business day means any day other than a Sunday, Saturday, or holiday.

(7) Customer account means a commodity futures or option account carried on the books of the applicant or registrant which is either:

(i) An account that is included in the definition of customer (as defined in §1.17(b)(2)), or

(ii) An account for a foreign-domiciled person trading on a foreign board of trade, where such account for the foreign-domiciled person is not a proprietary account (as defined in §1.17(b)(3)) or a noncustomer account (as defined in §1.17(b)(4)(ii)).

(8) Risk margin for an account means the level of maintenance margin or performance bond that the futures commission merchant is required to collect under the rules of an exchange, or the rules of a clearing organization if the level of margin to be collected is not determined by the rules of an exchange, from the owner of a customer account or noncustomer account, subject to the following:

(i) Risk margin does not include the equity component of short or long option positions maintained in an account;

(ii) The maintenance margin or performance bond requirement associated with a long option position may be excluded from risk margin to the extent that the value of such long option position does not reduce the total risk maintenance or performance bond requirement of the account that holds the long option position;

(iii) The risk margin for an account carried by a futures commission merchant which is not a member of the exchange or the clearing organization that requires collection of such margin should be calculated as if the futures commission merchant were such a member; and

(iv) If a futures commission merchant does not possess sufficient information to determine what portion of an account's total margin requirement represents risk margin, all of the margin required by the exchange or the clearing organization that requires collection of such margin for that account, shall be treated as risk margin.

(c) Definitions: For the purposes of this section:

(1) Net capital means the amount by which current assets exceed liabilities. In determining "net capital":

(i) Unrealized profits shall be added and unrealized losses shall be deducted in the accounts of the applicant or registrant, including unrealized profits and losses on fixed price commitments and forward contracts;

(ii) All long and all short positions in commodity options which are traded on a contract market and listed security options shall be marked to their market value and all long and all short securities and commodities positions shall be marked to their market value;

(iii) The value attributed to any commodity option which is not traded on a contract market shall be the difference between the option's strike price and the market value for the physical or futures contract which is the subject of the option. In the case of a call commodity option which is not traded on a contract market, if the market value for the physical or futures contract which is the subject of the option is less than the strike price of the option, it shall be given no value. In the case of a put commodity option which is not traded on a contract market, if the market value for the physical or futures contract which is the subject of the option is more than the strike price of the option, it shall be given no value; and

(iv) The value attributed to any unlisted security option shall be the difference between the option's exercise value or striking value and the market value of the underlying security. In the case of an unlisted call, if the market value of the underlying security is less than the exercise value or striking value of such call, it shall be given no value; and, in the case of an unlisted put, if the market value of the underlying security is more than the exercise value or striking value of the unlisted put, it shall be given no value.

(2) The term current assets means cash and other assets or resources commonly identified as those which are reasonably expected to be realized in cash or sold during the next 12 months. "Current assets" shall:

(i) Exclude any unsecured commodity futures or option account containing a ledger balance and open trades, the combination of which liquidates to a deficit or containing a debit ledger balance only: Provided, however, Deficits or debit ledger balances in unsecured customers', non-customers', and proprietary accounts, which are the subject of calls for margin or other required deposits may be included in current assets until the close of business on the business day following the date on which such deficit or debit ledger balance originated providing that the account had timely satisfied, through the deposit of new funds, the previous day's debit or deficits, if any, in its entirety.

(ii) Exclude all unsecured receivables, advances and loans except for:

(A) Receivables resulting from the marketing of inventories commonly associated with the business activities of the applicant or registrant and advances on fixed price purchases commitments: Provided, Such receivables or advances are outstanding no longer than 3 calendar months from the date that they are accrued;

(B) Interest receivable, floor brokerage receivable, commissions receivable from other brokers or dealers (other than syndicate profits), mutual fund concessions receivable and management fees receivable from registered investment companies and commodity pools: Provided, Such receivables are outstanding no longer than thirty (30) days from the date they are due; and dividends receivable outstanding no longer than thirty (30) days from the payable date;

(C) Receivables from clearing organizations and securities clearing organizations;

(D) Receivables from registered futures commission merchants or brokers, resulting from commodity futures or option transactions, except those specifically excluded under paragraph (c)(2)(i) of this section;

(E) Insurance claims which arise from a reportable segment of the applicant's or registrant's overall business activities, as defined in generally accepted accounting principles, other than in the commodity futures, commodity option, security and security option segments of the applicant's or registrant's business activities which are not outstanding more than 3 calendar months after the date they are recorded as a receivable;

(F) All other insurance claims not subject to paragraph (c)(2)(ii)(E) of this section, which are not older than seven (7) business days from the date the loss giving rise to the claim is discovered; insurance claims which are not older than twenty (20) business days from the date the loss giving rise to the claim is discovered and which are covered by an option of outside counsel that the claim is valid and is covered by insurance policies presently in effect; insurance claims which are older than twenty (20) business days from the date the loss giving rise to the claim is discovered and which are covered by an opinion of outside counsel that the claim is valid and is covered by insurance policies presently in effect and which have been acknowledged in writing by the insurance carrier as due and payable: Provided, Such claims are not outstanding longer than twenty (20) business days from the date they are so acknowledged by the carrier;

(iii) Exclude all prepaid expenses and deferred charges;

(iv) Exclude all inventories except for:

(A) Readily marketable spot commodities; or spot commodities which "adequately collateralize" indebtedness under paragraph (c)(7) of this section;

(B) Securities which are considered "readily marketable" (as defined in §240.15c3–1(c)(11) of this title) or which "adequately collateralize" indebtedness under paragraph (c)(7) of this section;

(C) Work in process and finished goods which result from the processing of commodities at market value;

(D) Raw materials at market value which will be combined with spot commodities to produce a finished processed commodity; and

(E) Inventories held for resale commonly associated with the business activities of the applicant or registrant;

(v) Include fixed assets and assets which otherwise would be considered noncurrent to the extent of any long-term debt adequately collateralized by assets acquired for use in the ordinary course of the trade or business of an applicant or registrant and any other long-term debt adequately collateralized by assets of the applicant or registrant if the sole recourse of the creditor for nonpayment of such liability is to such asset: Provided, Such liabilities are not excluded from liabilities in the computation of net capital under paragraph (c)(4)(vi) of this section;

(vi) Exclude all assets doubtful of collection or realization less any reserves established therefore;

(vii) Include, in the case of future income tax benefits arising as a result of unrealized losses, the amount of such benefits not exceeding the amount of income tax liabilities accrued on the books and records of the applicant or registrant, but only to the extent such benefits could have been applied to reduce accrued tax liabilities on the date of the capital computation, had the related unrealized losses been realized on that date;

(viii) Include guarantee deposits with clearing organizations and stock in clearing organizations to the extent of its margin value;

(ix) In the case of an introducing broker or an applicant for registration as an introducing broker, include 50 percent of the value of a guarantee or security deposit with a futures commission merchant which carries or intends to carry accounts for the customers of the introducing broker; and

(x) Exclude exchange memberships.

(3) A loan or advance or any other form of receivable shall not be considered "secured" for the purposes of paragraph (c)(2) of this section unless the following conditions exist:

(i) The receivable is secured by readily marketable collateral which is otherwise unencumbered and which can be readily converted into cash: Provided, however, That the receivable will be considered secured only to the extent of the market value of such collateral after application of the percentage deductions specified in paragraph (c)(5) of this section; and

(ii)(A) The readily marketable collateral is in the possession or control of the applicant or registrant; or

(B) The applicant or registrant has a legally enforceable, written security agreement, signed by the debtor, and has a perfected security interest in the readily marketable collateral within the meaning of the laws of the State in which the readily marketable collateral is located.

(4) The term liabilities means the total money liabilities of an applicant or registrant arising in connection with any transaction whatsoever, including economic obligations of an applicant or registrant that are recognized and measured in conformity with generally accepted accounting principles. "Liabilities" also include certain deferred credits that are not obligations but that are recognized and measured in conformity with generally accepted accounting principles. For the purposes of computing "net capital," the term "liabilities":

(i) Excludes liabilities of an applicant or registrant which are subordinated to the claims of all general creditors of the applicant or registrant pursuant to a satisfactory subordination agreement, as defined in paragraph (h) of this section;

(ii) Excludes, in the case of a futures commission merchant, the amount of money, securities and property due to commodity futures or option customers which is held in segregated accounts in compliance with the requirements of the Act and these regulations: Provided, however, That such exclusion may be taken only if such money, securities and property held in segregated accounts have been excluded from current assets in computing net capital;

(iii) Includes, in the case of an applicant or registrant who is a sole proprietor, the excess of liabilities which have not been incurred in the course of business as a futures commission merchant or as an introducing broker over assets not used in the business;

(iv) Excludes the lesser of any deferred income tax liability related to the items in paragraphs (c)(4)(i) (A), (B), and (C) below, or the sum of paragraphs (c)(4)(i) (A), (B), and (C) below:

(A) The aggregate amount resulting from applying to the amount of the deductions computed in accordance with paragraph (c)(5) of this section the appropriate Federal and State tax rate(s) applicable to any unrealized gain on the asset on which the deduction was computed;

(B) Any deferred tax liability related to income accrued which is directly related to an asset otherwise deducted pursuant to this section;

(C) Any deferred tax liability related to unrealized appreciation in value of any asset(s) which has been otherwise excluded from current assets in accordance with the provisions of this section;

(v) Excludes any current tax liability related to income accrued which is directly related to an asset otherwise deducted pursuant to this section; and

(vi) Excludes liabilities which would be classified as long term in accordance with generally accepted accounting principles to the extent of the net book value of plant, property and equipment which is used in the ordinary course of any trade or business of the applicant or registrant which is a reportable segment of the applicant's or registrant's overall business activities, as defined in generally accepted accounting principles, other than in the commodity futures, commodity option, security and security option segments of the applicant's or registrant's business activities: Provided, That such plant, property and equipment is not included in current assets pursuant to paragraph (c)(2)(v) of this section.

(5) The term adjusted net capital means net capital less:

(i) The amount by which any advances paid by the applicant or registrant on cash commodity contracts and used in computing net capital exceeds 95 percent of the market value of the commodities covered by such contracts;

(ii) In the case of all inventory, fixed price commitments and forward contracts, the applicable percentage of the net position specified below:

(A) Inventory which is currently registered as deliverable on a contract market and covered by an open futures contract or by a commodity option on a physical.—No charge.

(B) Inventory which is covered by an open futures contract or commodity option.—5 percent of the market value.

(C) Inventory which is not covered.—20 percent of the market value.

(D) Inventory and forward contracts in those foreign currencies that are purchased or sold for future delivery on or subject to the rules of a contract market, and which are covered by an open futures contract.—No charge

(E) Inventory and forward contracts in euros, British pounds, Canadian dollars, Japanese yen, or Swiss francs, and which are not covered by an open futures contract or commodity option.—6 percent of the market value.

(F) Fixed price commitments (open purchases and sales) and forward contracts which are covered by an open futures contract or commodity option.—10 percent of the market value.

(G) Fixed price commitments (open purchases and sales) and forward contracts which are not covered by an open futures contract or commodity option.—20 percent of the market value.

(iii)–(iv) [Reserved]

(v) In the case of securities and obligations used by the applicant or registrant in computing net capital, and in the case of a futures commission merchant with securities in segregation pursuant to section 4d(2) of the Act and the regulations in this chapter which were not deposited by customers, the percentages specified in Rule 240.15c3–1(c)(2)(vi) of the Securities and Exchange Commission (17 CFR 240.15c3–1(c)(2)(vi)) ("securities haircuts") and 100 percent of the value of "non-marketable securities" as specified in Rule 240.15c3–1(c)(2)(vii) of the Securities and Exchange Commission (17 CFR 240.15c3–1(c)(2)(vii));

(vi) In the case of securities options and/or other options for which a haircut has been specified for the option or for the underlying instrument in §240.15c3–1 appendix A of this title, the treatment specified in, or under, §240.15c3−1 appendix A, after effecting certain adjustments to net capital for listed and unlisted options as set forth in such appendix;

(vii) In the case of an applicant or registrant who has open contractual commitments, as hereinafter defined, the deductions specified in §240.15c3−1(c)(2)(viii) of this title;

(viii) In the case of a futures commission merchant, for undermargined customer commodity futures accounts and commodity option customer accounts the amount of funds required in each such account to meet maintenance margin requirements of the applicable board of trade or if there are no such maintenance margin requirements, clearing organization margin requirements applicable to such positions, after application of calls for margin or other required deposits which are outstanding three business days or less. If there are no such maintenance margin requirements or clearing organization margin requirements, then the amount of funds required to provide margin equal to the amount necessary after application of calls for margin or other required deposits outstanding three business days or less to restore original margin when the original margin has been depleted by 50 percent or more: Provided, To the extent a deficit is excluded from current assets in accordance with paragraph (c)(2)(i) of this section such amount shall not also be deducted under this paragraph (c)(5)(viii). In the event that an owner of a customer account has deposited an asset other than cash to margin, guarantee or secure his account, the value attributable to such asset for purposes of this subparagraph shall be the lesser of (A) the value attributable to the asset pursuant to the margin rules of the applicable board of trade, or (B) the market value of the asset after application of the percentage deductions specified in this paragraph (c)(5);

(ix) In the case of a futures commission merchant, for undermargined commodity futures and commodity option noncustomer and omnibus accounts the amount of funds required in each such account to meet maintenance margin requirements of the applicable board of trade or if there are no such maintenance margin requirements, clearing organization margin requirements applicable to such positions, after application of calls for margin or other required deposits which are outstanding two business days or less. If there are no such maintenance margin requirements or clearing organization margin requirements, then the amount of funds required to provide margin equal to the amount necessary after application of calls for margin or other required deposits outstanding two business days or less to restore original margin when the original margin has been depleted by 50 percent or more: Provided, To the extent a deficit is excluded from current assets in accordance with paragraph (c)(2)(i) of this section such amount shall not also be deducted under this paragraph (c)(5)(ix). In the event that an owner of a noncustomer or omnibus account has deposited an asset other than cash to margin, guarantee or secure his account the value attributable to such asset for purposes of this subparagraph shall be the lesser of (A) the value attributable to such asset pursuant to the margin rules of the applicable board of trade, or (B) the market value of such asset after application of the percentage deductions specified in this paragraph (c)(5);

(x) In the case of open futures contracts and granted (sold) commodity options held in proprietary accounts carried by the applicant or registrant which are not covered by a position held by the applicant or registrant or which are not the result of a "changer trade" made in accordance with the rules of a contract market:

(A) For an applicant or registrant which is a clearing member of a clearing organization for the positions cleared by such member, the applicable margin requirement of the applicable clearing organization;

(B) For an applicant or registrant which is a member of a self-regulatory organization 150 percent of the applicable maintenance margin requirement of the applicable board of trade, or clearing organization, whichever is greater;

(C) For all other applicants or registrants, 200 percent of the applicable maintenance margin requirements of the applicable board of trade or clearing organization, whichever is greater; or

(D) For open contracts or granted (sold) commodity options for which there are no applicable maintenance margin requirements, 200 percent of the applicable initial margin requirement: Provided, The equity in any such proprietary account shall reduce the deduction required by this paragraph (c)(5)(x) if such equity is not otherwise includable in adjusted net capital;

(xi) In the case of an applicant or registrant which is a purchaser of a commodity option not traded on a contract market which has value and such value is used to increase adjusted net capital, ten percent of the market value of the physical or futures contract which is the subject of such option but in no event more than the value attributed to such option;

(xii) In the case of an applicant or registrant which is a purchaser of a commodity option which is traded on a contract market the same safety factor as if the applicant or registrant were the grantor of such option in accordance with paragraph (c)(5)(x) of this section, but in no event shall the safety factor be greater than the market value attributed to such option;

(xiii) Five percent of all unsecured receivables includable under paragraph (c)(2)(ii)(D) of this section used by the applicant or registrant in computing "net capital" and which are not due from:

(A) A registered futures commission merchant;

(B) A broker or dealer that is registered as such with the Securities and Exchange Commission; or

(C) A foreign broker that has been granted comparability relief pursuant to §30.10 of this chapter, Provided, however, that the amount of the unsecured receivable not subject to the five percent capital charge is no greater than 150 percent of the current amount required to maintain futures and option positions in accounts with the foreign broker, or 100 percent of such greater amount required to maintain futures and option positions in the accounts at any time during the previous six-month period, and Provided, that, in the case of customer funds, such account is treated in accordance with the special requirements of the applicable Commission order issued under §30.10 of this chapter.

(xiv) For securities brokers and dealers, all other deductions specified in §240.15c3–1 of this title.

(6) Election of alternative capital deductions that have received approval of Securities and Exchange Commission pursuant to §240.15c3–1(a)(7) of this title.

(i) Any futures commission merchant that is also registered with the Securities and Exchange Commission as a securities broker or dealer, and who also satisfies the other requirements of this paragraph (c)(6), may elect to compute its adjusted net capital using the alternative capital deductions that, under §240.15c3–1(a)(7) of this title, the Securities and Exchange Commission has approved by written order. To the extent that a futures commission merchant is permitted by the Securities and Exchange Commission to use alternative capital deductions for its unsecured receivables from over-the-counter transactions in derivatives, or for its proprietary positions in securities, forward contracts, or futures contracts, the futures commission merchant may use these same alternative capital deductions when computing its adjusted net capital, in lieu of the deductions that would otherwise be required by paragraph (c)(2)(ii) of this section for its unsecured receivables from over-the-counter derivatives transactions; by paragraph (c)(5)(ii) of this section for its proprietary positions in forward contracts; by paragraph (c)(5)(v) of this section for its proprietary positions in securities; and by paragraph (c)(5)(x) of this section for its proprietary positions in futures contracts.

(ii) Notifications of election or of changes to election. (A) No election to use the alternative market risk and credit risk deductions referenced in paragraph (c)(6)(i) of this section shall be effective unless and until the futures commission merchant has filed with the Commission, addressed to the Director of the Division of Clearing and Intermediary Oversight, a notice that is to include a copy of the approval order of the Securities and Exchange Commission referenced in paragraph (c)(6)(i) of this section, and to include also a statement that identifies the amount of tentative net capital below which the futures commission merchant is required to provide notice to the Securities and Exchange Commission, and which also provides the following information: a list of the categories of positions that the futures commission merchant holds in its proprietary accounts, and, for each such category, a description of the methods that the futures commission merchant will use to calculate its deductions for market risk and credit risk, and also, if calculated separately, deductions for specific risk; a description of the value at risk (VaR) models to be used for its market risk and credit risk deductions, and an overview of the integration of the models into the internal risk management control system of the futures commission merchant; a description of how the futures commission merchant will calculate current exposure and maximum potential exposure for its deductions for credit risk; a description of how the futures commission merchant will determine internal credit ratings of counterparties and internal credit risk weights of counterparties, if applicable; and a description of the estimated effect of the alternative market risk and credit risk deductions on the amounts reported by the futures commission merchant as net capital and adjusted net capital.

(B) A futures commission merchant must also, upon the request of the Commission at any time, supplement the statement described in paragraph (c)(6)(ii)(A) of this section, by providing any other explanatory information regarding the computation of its alternative market risk and credit risk deductions as the Commission may require at its discretion.

(C) A futures commission merchant must also file the following supplemental notices with the Director of the Division and Clearing and Intermediary Oversight:

(1) A notice advising that the Securities and Exchange Commission has imposed additional or revised conditions for the approval evidenced by the order referenced in paragraph (c)(6)(i) of this section, and which describes the new or revised conditions in full, and

(2) A notice which attaches a copy of any approval by the Securities and Exchange Commission of amendments that a futures commission merchant has requested for its application, filed under 17 CFR 240.15c3–1e, to use alternative market risk and credit risk deductions approved by the Securities and Exchange Commission.

(D) A futures commission merchant may voluntarily change its election to use the alternative market risk and credit risk deductions referenced in paragraph (c)(6)(i) of this section, by filing with the Director of the Division of Clearing and Intermediary Oversight a written notice specifying a future date as of which it will no longer use the alternative market risk and credit risk deductions, and will instead compute such deductions in accordance with the requirements otherwise applicable under paragraph (c)(2)(ii) of this section for unsecured receivables from over-the-counter derivatives transactions; by paragraph (c)(5)(ii) of this section for proprietary positions in forward contracts; by paragraph (c)(5)(v) of this section for proprietary positions in securities; and by paragraph (c)(5)(x) of this section for proprietary positions in futures contracts.

(iii) Conditions under which election terminated. A futures commission merchant may no longer elect to use the alternative market risk and credit risk deductions referenced in paragraph (c)(6)(i) of this section, and shall instead compute the deductions otherwise required under paragraph (c)(2)(ii) of this section for unsecured receivables from over-the-counter derivatives transactions; by paragraph (c)(5)(ii) of this section for proprietary positions in forward contracts; by paragraph (c)(5)(v) of this section for proprietary positions in securities; and by paragraph (c)(5)(x) of this section for proprietary positions in futures contracts, upon the occurrence of any of the following:

(A) The Securities and Exchange Commission revokes its approval of the market risk and credit risk deductions for such futures commission merchant;

(B) A futures commission merchant fails to come into compliance with its filing requirements under this paragraph (c)(6), after having received from the Director of the Division of Clearing and Intermediary Oversight written notification that the firm is not in compliance with its filing requirements, and must cease using alternative capital deductions permitted under this paragraph (c)(6) if it has not come into compliance by a date specified in the notice; or

(C) The Commission by written order finds that permitting the futures commission merchant to continue to use such alternative market risk and credit risk deductions is no longer necessary or appropriate for the protection of customers of the futures commission merchant or of the integrity of the futures or options markets.

(iv) Additional filing requirements. Any futures commission merchant that elects to use the alternative market risk and credit risk deductions referenced in paragraph (c)(6)(i) of this section must file with the Commission, in addition to the filings required by paragraph (c)(6)(ii) of this section, copies of any and all of the following documents, at such time as the originals are filed with the Securities and Exchange Commission:

(A) Information that the futures commission merchant files on a monthly basis with its designated examining authority or the Securities and Exchange Commission, whether by way of schedules to its FOCUS reports or by other filings, in satisfaction of 17 CFR 240.17a–5(a)(5)(i);

(B) The quarterly reports required by 17 CFR 240.17a–5(a)(5)(ii);

(C) The supplemental annual filings as required by 17 CFR 240.17a–5(k);

(D) Any notification to the Securities and Exchange Commission or the futures commission merchant's designated examining authority of planned withdrawals of excess net capital; and

(E) Any notification that the futures commission merchant is required to file with the Securities and Exchange Commission when its tentative net capital is below an amount specified by the Securities and Exchange Commission.

(7) Liabilities are "adequately collateralized" when, pursuant to a legally enforceable written instrument, such liabilities are secured by identified assets that are otherwise unencumbered and the market value of which exceeds the amount of such liabilities.

(8) The term contractual commitments shall include underwriting, when issued, when distributed, and delayed delivery contracts; and the writing or endorsement of security puts and calls and combinations thereof; but shall not include uncleared

regular way purchases and sales of securities. A series of contracts of purchase or sale of the same security, conditioned, if at all, only upon issuance, may be treated as an individual commitment.

(d) Each applicant or registrant shall have equity capital (inclusive of satisfactory subordination agreements which qualify under this paragraph (d) as equity capital) of not less than 30 percent of the debt-equity total, provided, an applicant or registrant may be exempted from the provisions of this paragraph (d) for a period not to exceed 90 days or for such longer period which the Commission may, upon application of the applicant or registrant, grant in the public interest or for the protection of investors. For the purposes of this paragraph (d):

(1) Equity capital means a satisfactory subordination agreement entered into by a partner or stockholder or limited liability company member which has an initial term of at least 3 years and has a remaining term of not less than 12 months if:

(i) It does not have any of the provisions for accelerated maturity provided for by paragraphs (h)(2) (ix)(A), (x)(A), or (x)(B) of this section, or the provisions allowing for special prepayment provided for by paragraph (h)(2)(vii)(B) of this section, and is maintained as capital subject to the provisions restricting the withdrawal thereof required by paragraph (e) of this section; or

(ii) The partnership agreement provides that capital contributed pursuant to a satisfactory subordination agreement as defined in paragraph (h) of this section shall in all respects be partnership capital subject to the provisions restricting the withdrawal thereof required by paragraph (e) of this section, and

(A) In the case of a corporation, the sum of its par or stated value of capital stock, paid in capital in excess of par, retained earnings, unrealized profit and loss, and other capital accounts.

(B) In the case of a partnership, the sum of its capital accounts of partners (inclusive of such partners' commodities, options and securities accounts subject to the provisions of paragraph (e) of this section), and unrealized profit and loss.

(C) In the case of a sole proprietorship, the sum of its capital accounts of the sole proprietorship and unrealized profit and loss.

(D) In the case of a limited liability company, the sum of its capital accounts of limited liability company members, and unrealized profit and loss. (A)

(2) Debt-equity total means equity capital as defined in paragraph (d)(1) of this section L) plus the outstanding principal amount of satisfactory subordination agreements. E

(e) No equity capital of the applicant or registrant or a subsidiary's or affiliate's equity x capital consolidated pursuant to paragraph (f) of this section, whether in the form of (A) capital contributions by partners (including amounts in the commodities, options and n securities trading accounts of partners which are treated as equity capital but excluding d amounts in such trading accounts which are not equity capital and excluding balances (R) in limited partners' capital accounts in excess of their stated capital contributions), par A or stated value of capital stock, paid-in capital in excess of par or stated value, retained earnings or other capital accounts, may be withdrawn by action of a stockholder or partner or limited liability company member or by redemption or repurchase of shares of stock by any of the consolidated entities or through the payment of dividends or any similar distribution, nor may any unsecured advance or loan be made to a stockholder, partner, sole proprietor, limited liability company member, or employee if, after giving effect thereto and to any other such withdrawals, advances, or loans and any payments of payment obligations (as defined in paragraph (h) of this section) under satisfactory subordination agreements and any payments of liabilities excluded pursuant to paragraph (c)(4)(vi) of this section which are scheduled to occur within six months following such withdrawal, advance or loan:

(1) Either adjusted net capital of any of the consolidated entities would be less than the greatest of:

(i) 120 percent of the appropriate minimum dollar amount required by paragraphs (a)(1)(i)(A) or (a)(1)(iii)(A) of this section;

(ii) For a futures commission merchant or applicant therefor, 120 percent of the amount required by paragraph (a)(1)(i)(B) of this section;

(iii) 120 percent of the amount of adjusted net capital required by a registered futures association of which it is a member; or

(iv) For an applicant or registrant which is also a securities broker or dealer, the amount of net capital specified in Rule 15c3–1(e) of the Securities and Exchange Commission (17 CFR 240.15c3–1(e)); or

(2) In the case of any applicant or registrant included within such consolidation, if equity capital of the applicant or registrant (inclusive of satisfactory subordination agreements which qualify as equity under paragraph (d) of this section) would be less than 30 percent of the required debt-equity total as defined in paragraph (d) of this section.

Provided, That this paragraph (e) shall not preclude an applicant or registrant from making required tax payments or preclude the payment to partners of reasonable compensation. The Commission may, upon application of the applicant or registrant, grant relief from this paragraph (e) if the Commission deems it to be in the public interest or for the protection of nonproprietary accounts.

(Approved by the Office of Management and Budget under control number 3038–0024)

[43 FR 39972, Sept. 8, 1978]

Index

Index compiled by Terry Halliday